Using Characters and Themes to Inspire Early Learning

Offering an approach that is tried, tested and proven to work, this book supports practitioners in planning and resourcing a series of topics based around popular themes and interests in the early years. Each topic is open-ended and introduced in the form of a problem that the children have to solve and can be led by their knowledge, thoughts and ideas.

Using Characters and Themes to Inspire Early Learning aims to nurture children's natural curiosity and imagination, encouraging them to become the facilitators who are empowered to solve problems, explore solutions and take ownership of their learning.

There are links throughout to the seven areas of learning in the EYFS and practical guidance on how to document the children's learning. Features include:

- An exciting range of characters, themes and objects to inspire children.

- Photocopiable pages and online resources to use in the classroom.

- Session breakdowns to set the scene and make planning easy.

- Creative ideas and activities to prompt children's thinking and develop discussions.

Packed with ideas for extending learning and practical resources that can be printed out for use in the classroom, this book is essential reading for all students and practitioners who want to provide inspiring learning opportunities for the children in their care.

Jo Ayers and **Louise Robson** are Reception teachers and early years consultants, UK. They provide practical support to schools and early years settings in delivering the Early Years Foundation Stage, phonics and literacy.

Using Characters and Themes to Inspire Early Learning

A practical guide

**Jo Ayers and
Louise Robson**

Routledge
Taylor & Francis Group

LONDON AND NEW YORK

First published 2017
by Routledge
2 Park Square, Milton Park, Abingdon, Oxon OX14 4RN

and by Routledge
711 Third Avenue, New York, NY 10017

Routledge is an imprint of the Taylor & Francis Group, an informa business

© 2017 Jo Ayers and Louise Robson

British Library Cataloguing in Publication Data
A catalogue record for this book is available from the British Library

Library of Congress Cataloging in Publication Data
A catalog record for this book has been requested

ISBN: 978-1-138-69614-3 (hbk)
ISBN: 978-1-138-69615-0 (pbk)
ISBN: 978-1-315-52529-7 (ebk)

Typeset in Helvetica & Garamond Three
by Florence Production Ltd, Stoodleigh, Devon, UK

Visit the eResources: www.routledge.com/9781138696150

Contents

Acknowledgements

We would like to thank the wonderful children from the various settings we have worked in. Thank you for always inspiring us to innovate our teaching approaches and for embracing our characters with such enthusiasm.

Thank you to our publishers for making our dreams of a book into a reality.

And finally, a huge thank you to Ian Ward our illustrator for bringing the characters we have so long imagined, to life.

Introduction

The aim of this book is to provide ideas and resources to support the delivery of topics based around popular interests and themes in the early years. It is designed specifically for educators working with children aged 3–5 years and meets all the EYFS expectations.

The authors have worked in early years education for over 10 years and have successfully used the material included to obtain outstanding results and gradings during their last two Ofsted inspections (latest one October 2014 under the new requirements). The settings they have worked in are larger than average-sized primary schools where children enter the setting with weak early language skills and social development and consistently make excellent progress to achieve inline or above the national average levels of attainment in all areas.

The book includes ideas, resources and examples to help develop the project and the work done by the children.

The aim of *Using Characters and Themes to Inspire Early Learning* is to provide practitioners with suggestions for setting up the projects; inspiring, open-ended resources that can accompany their planning; and practical ways to document this learning.

There is a strong emphasis on involving children in the planning process, which allows them to take ownership of their learning.

THE THEMES

The book is subdivided into varying topics based on some of the children's interests and passions. These are all linked to the seven different areas of learning to be covered in the Foundation Stage: Personal, Social and Emotional Development, Communication and Language, Physical Development, Literacy, Mathematics, Understanding the World and Expressive Arts and Design.

Each topic includes a starting point that will capture and inspire the children's imaginations. If there is not a topic here you feel your children will enjoy, it may give you the inspiration to try these ideas with a theme of your own. You could also adapt the characters and themes to suit your cohort of children.

Alongside each topic, you will need to teach discrete sessions of phonics and mathematics to ensure all aspects of the EYFS goals are covered.

PLANNING

Before you begin any topics, gather the children together and ask them about their favourite interests. You can always send out a questionnaire and include parents in the planning process too.

The planning has been broken down into sessions. You may find that some aspects of the topic take longer than others, especially if the children really become engrossed in a specific element of the planning. Not all seven areas of learning will be covered every session but across the topic objectives from all seven areas of learning will be covered. Personal, Social and Emotional Development and Communication and Language will be covered throughout the topics so may not be specifically planned out in each chapter, but objectives can be highlighted for these areas in retrospect.

While you are gathering evidence, use a variety of methods, including children's work, their comments, Post-it note observations, photographs, recordings, etc.

QUESTIONING

It is your role as the teacher to guide and scaffold the project. The children will lead some of the learning through ideas and interests, but ultimately it is your role to extend their learning and help them to elaborate on their ideas. Use open-ended questions such as: Who do the items belong to? How did they get here? Why do you think that? What could we do next? How can we solve this problem?

To begin with, you may need to give your children more hints and support to come up with ideas and solutions. As they become more accustomed and confident in this topic approach, they will surprise you and come up with ideas you never even thought of!

PERSONAL, SOCIAL AND EMOTIONAL DEVELOPMENT

The feelings of the characters can be incorporated into discussions. For example, Sammy the Sports Car is in a position where he experiences worries and upset. This is a good opportunity for empathy to be encouraged and developed in a safe learning environment. Also, the concept of helping someone else who is in trouble is an important skill to develop.

Teamwork and collaboration are vital skills and are central to such an approach to learning. A variety of objectives will be covered in this manner.

Child-initiated tasks also encourage children to choose the resources they need and want to use to complete their task successfully. They are encouraged to evaluate and adapt their work as appropriate.

The open-ended, child-led approach developed in this book encourages critical thinking, independence, motivation and engagement.

COMMUNICATION AND LANGUAGE

The whole approach embraces the need for discussion and explanation, negotiating and reasoning, and justifying thoughts and ideas.

Talk partners can be set up to extend the speaking and listening further. These can work very well, and it is up to you how best to set these up (for example, ability pairs, set pairings based on who works well together, speak to the person next to you, etc.). Give children an amount of time to talk; the length of this will depend on the question or problem that you have asked them to discuss. When asking children for feedback, ask them to share what their partner thought to ensure they listen to each other rather than having one child dominate the conversation.

Central to this book is nurturing the children's natural curiosity and imagination. Each topic is open-ended and can be led by the children's own knowledge, thoughts and ideas. The children themselves become the facilitators; they are the experts who are empowered to solve problems and explore solutions based around their interests and characters they are familiar with.

So be brave and go and explore! The only limitations are your imagination.

CHAPTER 1

Sammy the Sports Car

SETTING THE SCENE

Scenario plot

This is the storyline that runs throughout the project. As the children will lead some of the learning through their thoughts and ideas, feel free to change or adapt the storyline if necessary.

Session 1

Setting the scene using mystery objects. The children use their prior knowledge to investigate who these items might belong to. A letter arrives explaining Sammy needs to be diverted but has become lost. Can the children help him get back home?

Session 2

A mock news report is shown discussing the devastation caused by the flooding. Children must help to repair the tracks from flood damage so that the Axel Cup races can go ahead.

Session 3

A poster advertising the races appears in the classroom, but it states that the event has had to be cancelled despite the children's best efforts. The children decide upon a new venue and plan and organise the races to be held there.

Session 4

Race-day! Children set up for the races and hold their own Axel Cup championships to find a winner.

SESSION 1: STARTING POINTS

The spark!

A set of mysterious objects appear on the carpet. The children then discuss who they might belong to and why they are there. We used items shown in the photograph plus a selection of resources from Appendix 1.1.

★ This is a good opportunity to introduce talk partners. Can the children listen to others and take turns sharing ideas?

★ Encourage the children to think of reasons for their responses. This encourages critical thinking and reasoning skills to be developed.

Figure 1.1 *An example of artefacts you might like to use.*

What next?

After this initial discussion, it is now time to add in more detail to prompt the children's thinking. Share the letter from Appendix 1.2. The letter could be discovered hidden among the items you have found or brought into the classroom as a special delivery to add in a little more drama! This is a vital part of the project, so ensure that you share the letter slowly and clearly, ensuring that you give the children time to respond to the news they have received.

Create awe and wonder!

It is important that you immerse yourself in the role of facilitator to make this as realistic as possible for the children. The more enthusiastic you are, the more enthusiastic the children will become.

And then . . .

Create a list with the children. Record their ideas about what they already know about cars.

REMEMBER

Here, the children become the experts and often know more than you can ever imagine! Even the quietest children feel motivated and confident to share their knowledge if it is on a subject they feel passionate about.

Planning with the children

Develop the discussion into planning ways that they can help to solve the dilemma. If your children are new to this process, you may need to prompt ideas, but they will soon grasp the idea and lead their own learning. As you do more of this, their ideas will become more extensive and imaginative.

Below is a mind map of some possible activities that could be provided on day 1 of the topic.

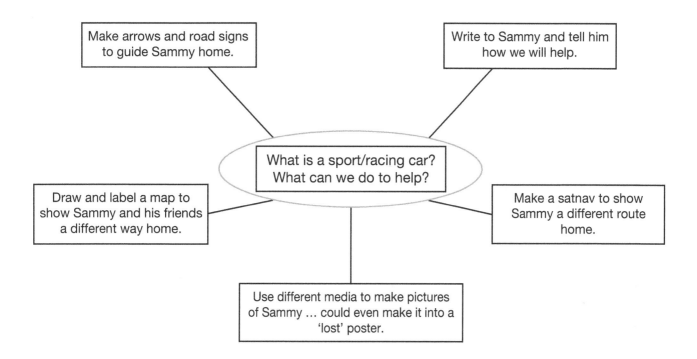

SESSION 2: THE FLOOD
======================

 **The spark!**

The children's curiosity and interest should now be ignited as today a message/video arrives in class (see script in Appendix 1.3). We have previously used this in the form of a mock news report, but you may like to use a letter, email or audio recording.

★ Planning for child-initiated learning can be daunting and requires some elements of freedom. You may not cover every area of learning every day, but across the topic all areas will be covered.

HOW CAN WE HELP?

Physical development

- Large-scale obstacle course to negotiate. Can the children find their way across to get to Sammy?

- Make bikes, trikes, etc. available for the children to explore.

Literacy

- Write messages to Sammy.

- Label maps and designs.

- Make list of what the children need to help Sammy.

Expressive Arts and Design

- Create a garage or car wash in your role-play area for the children to explore.

- Design and create their own models to get rid of the water (e.g. a giant vacuum to suck up all the floodwater).

Figure 1.2 The children may want to set up their own raceways in the outdoor area.

Understanding the world

- Make maps to show Sammy the way home – add on points of interest.

- Find out more about flooding and how the children could prevent it happening at Golden Park raceway again.

- Use programmable toys to follow a journey around Golden Park.

- Create their own news reports using video cameras, microphones, etc.

- Investigate floating and sinking and how the children can get the across the flood safely.

- Investigate waterproof materials to keep Sammy dry.

Figure 1.3 Here is a supercar designed to travel through the flood to get Sammy safely to the raceways.

SESSION 3: THE AXEL CUP

The spark!

Share the poster from Appendix 1.4. Although Sammy has arrived at Golden Park, the racetracks are now flooded and the Axel Cup has to be cancelled. Can the children suggest new venues?

The children can now discuss suitable venues and advantages and disadvantages for each. These will obviously differ according to the location of your school. Our children suggested:

- The park.

- The local shopping centre.

- The local go-karting track.

- Our school playground.

Try using this information to encourage the children to compile their own class surveys, graphs and questionnaires.

This then leads to a wealth of activities that the children can decide upon to get ready for the races.

NOTE

From this, the children may like to write to the head teacher to ask for help and advice. Our children decided to hold it in the school playground and asked our head teacher for permission and a time that would be convenient. You may decide on a local park or space available to you.

HOW CAN WE HELP?

PSED

- Look at how to be a 'good sport'.
- How can we be part of a team?

Literacy

- Write to the head teacher to ask permission.
- Plan what we need to prepare.
- Write lists of what we need to make/buy.
- Design and label supercars.
- Write to Sammy sharing the good news.

Mathematics

- Compile a class survey of favourite venues.
- Compile a traffic survey to discover the most popular car colour for their own designs.
- Wash the cars in preparation – encourage the children to use the language of capacity (e.g. full, empty).
- Order cars by size.
- Car number problems to solve.
- Design number plates.

Understanding the world

- Look at the types of racing cars we can design on the Internet.
- Record advertisements for the races using video cameras/microphones.
- Design posters using ICT programs.
- Investigate circuits to help fix the cars' lights.
- Use programmable toys to navigate around a racetrack.
- Investigate ramps and the impact they have on the speed of the cars.
- Investigate how a car works.

Expressive Arts and Design

- Make new supercars out of their chosen resources.
- Design their own raceways.
- Make helmets and costumes for the competitors.
- Make music to accompany their advertisement.

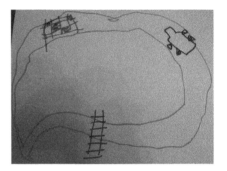

Figure 1.4 *A raceway design. This was then used by the child as a car mat as they added small-world cars and characters.*

Figure 1.5 *Cleaning the 'cars' so they are ready for the race-day.*

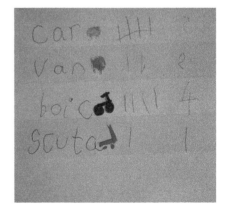

Figure 1.6 *Surveying our favourite mode of racing.*

SESSION 4: RACE-DAY

This is the day where the children need to prepare the area for the races. They need to get everything ready for the main event. Race-day is the culmination of all of their hard work and ideas. This is where the topic concludes and so it needs to be a spectacular event.

You may like to spend a session getting everything prepared and a different session holding the races themselves.

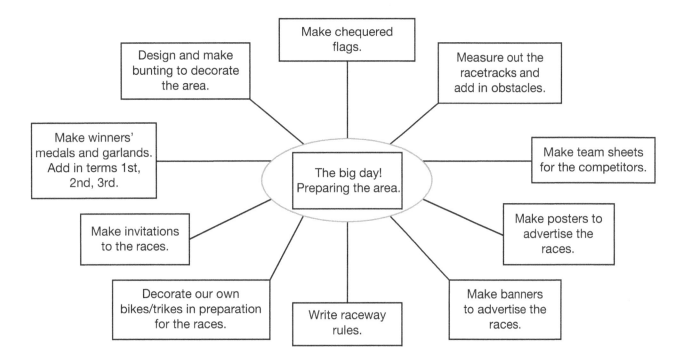

The big day!
Preparing the area.

- Make chequered flags.
- Design and make bunting to decorate the area.
- Measure out the racetracks and add in obstacles.
- Make winners' medals and garlands. Add in terms 1st, 2nd, 3rd.
- Make team sheets for the competitors.
- Make invitations to the races.
- Make posters to advertise the races.
- Decorate our own bikes/trikes in preparation for the races.
- Write raceway rules.
- Make banners to advertise the races.

Figure 1.7 *Making the new supercars.*

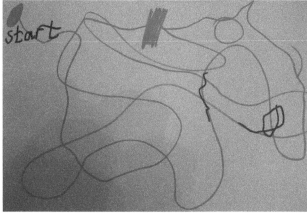

Figure 1.8 *A 'route' to follow to win the race! This child loved to role-play the races, carefully explaining the twists and turns.*

What next?

During the next session, the children receive a message from Sammy to say that unfortunately he cannot make it in time but has sent a trophy to say thank you for their help (see Appendix 1.5). This then leads nicely into the races themselves. You may like to divide the children into teams and use bikes/trikes/scooters to enact the races themselves. A grand winner may also be crowned.

Home links

Ask children to find out about their own cars. Can they bring in photos to share? Ask them to undertake a traffic survey in their street.

Visits out

- Try visiting a local garage to find out more about cars and the role of the mechanic.
- You may like to investigate your local area to look at the types of roads, traffic signs, lights, etc.
- You could invite in a local driving instructor to chat about how we need to learn to drive.
- This may lead into a road safety topic where you can look at crossing the road safely. Ask the school lollipop person to talk about road safety.

ENHANCED PROVISION

- Why not try turning your role play area into a garage?
- Add car magazines, road maps, car manuals and car-themed books to your library.
- Display keywords and character names around your classroom.
- Transfer the theme outdoors by opening a car wash or petrol station for the children to use with bikes and trikes.
- Use small-world versions of the characters to enhance play and storytelling.
- Add character-themed paper into every area – it is surprising how much incidental writing comes from just this small idea.
- Add tools, buckets, tyres and number plates to your building area.
- Use car-themed wrapping paper and stickers into your creative/making area.
- Enhance your classroom with simple car-themed party decorations. (These are fairly cheap and simple, but very inspiring!)

APPENDIX 1.2

Reception class, help me!

Yesterday, on our way home from our latest race, my friends and I were diverted along a different road! We couldn't go the usual way home and now we are completely lost. We don't know how to get back home now. We're not sure what the problem was at Golden Park raceways, but we desperately need some help.

Is there anything you can do?

Love from
Sammy the Sports Car

APPENDIX 1.3

NEWS READER:	Good evening and welcome to the 5 o'clock news. I'm Susan Smith. As we know, the Axel Cup is nearly upon us and everyone is very excited. However, at Golden Park, there has been mass flooding and this has led to several cars being stranded. We are highly concerned for the welfare of both those travelling to the event and the contestants. We're going live now to our reporter at Golden Park . . . Alison, I believe you have Sammy the Sports Car.
	(At the scene)
REPORTER:	Well hi Susan, yeah, here I am just outside Golden Park. We can't get any closer to the town as the roads are covered in water. I've found one of the top racing cars, Mr Sammy the Sports Car. So, Sammy, have you seen any of the flooding?
SAMMY:	Well, I saw all of the water covering the racetracks down in the valley; there's so much damage.
REPORTER:	Do you think the races will take place?
SAMMY:	Not here, not in Golden Park. The racetracks are completely flooded, they won't be dry in time.
REPORTER:	But what about the Axel Cup?
SAMMY:	I don't know! I don't know what we're going to do. Is there anyone that can help? I'm not sure, but I hope there is someone out there who can.
REPORTER:	Well, if there's anyone out there who can, there'll be a phone number on screen that you can call. Please phone if you have any ideas. We need to save the races.
	(Cut back to the studio)
NEWS READER:	Well, that's shocking news coming out of Golden Park. We really hope the Axel Cup can go ahead. Over to Zoe for the weather. I hope you have some good news for us; no one wants these races cancelled.

Hi, ... !

Thank you so much for all of your help; you have been wonderful. I need just one last favour: please can you help me advertise the race for this afternoon? People won't know where it is or how to get there. I'm really sorry, but there has been a problem at Ruby the Racing Car's hotel, so I need to stay in Golden Park to help her, but I look forward to hearing all about it. Perhaps you could send me some photographs and letters to let me know who wins!

Safe and happy racing!

Love from

Sammy the Sports Car

CHAPTER 2

The mysterious seed

SETTING THE SCENE

Session 1

Magical seeds are found somewhere in the classroom. The children use their prior knowledge to investigate where they are from, what they might grow into and how to care for them. Conclude the session with planting them.

Session 2

You will have created a magic beanstalk growing somewhere in the room. What has grown? What might be at the top? Later in the day, add on a bud to sustain interest.

Session 3

Add an arm or leg sticking out of the bud. Throughout the day, reveal more parts until the alien is fully revealed. How can we make the baby feel at home? How can we get him down and take care of him?

Session 4

A poster is found in the classroom. A mummy alien has lost her baby. Can we help her to get him back?

Session 5

A postcard explains that mummy and baby are reunited. Mummy has heard so much about earth but wants the children to find out more about space.

SESSION 1: STARTING POINTS

The spark!

Magical looking seeds are found somewhere in the classroom. A good time for this may be during snack time when the children can compare them to ones found in the fruit they may be eating. This is the starting point to a key discussion and will ignite the whole topic.

RESOURCES NEEDED

- large seeds such as pumpkin seeds
- paint
- glitter
- twigs
- pot
- soil
- alien toy

Let's discuss . . .

What have we found?

Where might they be from?

How can we care for them?

What might they grow into?

NOTE

Be creative when preparing your seeds. You could paint some shop-bought seeds silver or gold, or even dip them in glitter. It is vital that they look different to the everyday seeds your children may recognise.

Figure 2.1
We painted sweets in metallic colours.

What next?

These are the types of activities that may be provided during Session 1.

Compare the mysterious seeds to those in fruits/plants we recognise.

- Discuss how they are similar and different.

- Sort a variety of seeds by size/shape or colour. Do our seeds fit into these categories?

Make their own seed packets to protect the seeds.

- Look at a variety of seed packets and designing their own.

Make 'found' posters.

- Display posters around the classroom. The owner of the seeds may have lost them and need them back.

Draw/paint or write about what their seeds may grow into or who the owner may be.

- Here, the children may relate this to their own experiences. 'It might be Jack and they might grow into a beanstalk.' 'They might belong to my grandad, from his garden.'

Take care of the seeds until they grow.

- Discuss how we may help them grow. This may need guidance or research depending on the knowledge of your children. Once this is established, then you can plant the seeds and keep a simple class or individual seed diary (see Appendix 2.1).

Figure 2.1 *The children made seed packets to protect their magic seeds.*

SESSION 2: MAGIC BEANSTALK

Preparation

You will need to set up a giant beanstalk-type plant within the classroom. This may be dramatic in colour . . . silver, sparkly, spotty! The more imaginative, the better! We have used painted sticks and leaves or even padded out a pair of tights . . . try to ensure that the top of the plant disappears somehow . . . through a ceiling tile or out of a window.

Creating awe and wonder!

As the children enter the classroom, they will be 'wowed' as they notice how the seeds have grown overnight. Seize the moment by prompting a creative discussion: What has happened? What has grown? What might be at the top? You may like to create a thought shower (see Appendix 2.2). This can be continued throughout the topic.

And later in the day . . .

Add on a small bud, egg, box or flower. This sustains the suspense and continues the dialogue. It may lead to activities such as:

- Draw what might be inside.

- Make items to help look more closely at the bud (telescope binoculars).

- Discuss how we can care for the bud and how we can make it open.

- Record changes in a seed diary.

Figure 2.3 *We planted ours outdoors.*

SESSION 3: AN ALIEN APPEARS

The spark!

The children's curiosity and interest should now be ignited as today the bud is more open and a tiny arm or leg is sticking out. We have previously used an insect or alien toy or teddy. Throughout the day, more parts emerge until the alien/insect is fully revealed (see Figures 2.4–2.6).

Figure 2.4 *Something strange appeared at the top!*

Figure 2.5 *Out popped a leg!*

Figure 2.6 *. . . and another!*

Provoking thoughts

★ What is he/she? How do we know? Have we ever seen anything like this before?

★ Where could he/she be from?

★ How did he/she get here?

★ How does he/she feel? Have you ever felt scared?

★ What does a baby need to be cared for?

★ How can we help?

HOW CAN WE HELP?

Physical development

- Large-scale apparatus to develop children's climbing and hanging skills. Imagine they are rescuing the alien.

- Use large- and small-scale construction to design ways to rescue the alien.

Literacy

- Write messages to the alien.

- Make 'welcome to earth' cards.

- List how to care for a baby alien.

- Research space using class library/Internet.

- Make 'do not touch' signs to leave in the classroom overnight.

- Make 'found' posters to help find the alien's parents.

Expressive Arts and Design

- Create a class space rocket/space station.

- Design and create their own models to get the alien down safely – ladders, parachutes, slides and trampolines are usually popular.

- Design and make the alien a home.

- Make alien masks to make the baby feel safe.

- Make an alien friend.

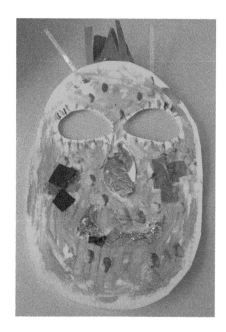

Figure 2.7 *'If we wear an alien mask, he won't be scared and he will come down!'*

PSNR

- Use the language of measurement to compare distances. How far is it to the top of the beanstalk? How can we measure?

- Survey our favourite names for the alien and create name tags.

Figure 2.8 *The children planned their own rocket models.*

Figure 2.9 *They then created them out of their own chosen materials.*

PSED

- Discuss how the baby may feel and how we can help make him feel better.

- Look at the needs of a baby and how this changes over time.

- Talk about how the alien is different to us but still special.

Understanding the world

- Discuss where the alien is from.

- Use ICT to record messages to the alien.

- Use laptops and PCs to find out more – this could be given as a family project to promote home-school links.

- Make alien food – green jelly, icing space biscuits.

- Create fact files to tell the alien more about our school and its rules.

- Generate rules to be a good earthling.

SESSION 4: LOST

The spark!

Share the poster from Appendix 2.3. You might like to hang it somewhere prominent in your setting for the children to find. Discuss the 'lost' poster from mummy alien and how you can help with her dilemma.

This then leads to a wealth of activities that the children can decide upon to get the baby alien home safely. Here are some examples of the ideas the children may generate.

Remember to provide open-ended resources to allow them to explore their ideas such as paper, boxes, construction.

REMEMBER

Planning for child-initiated learning can be daunting and requires some elements of freedom. You may not cover every area of learning every day, but across the topic all areas will be covered.

HOW CAN WE HELP?

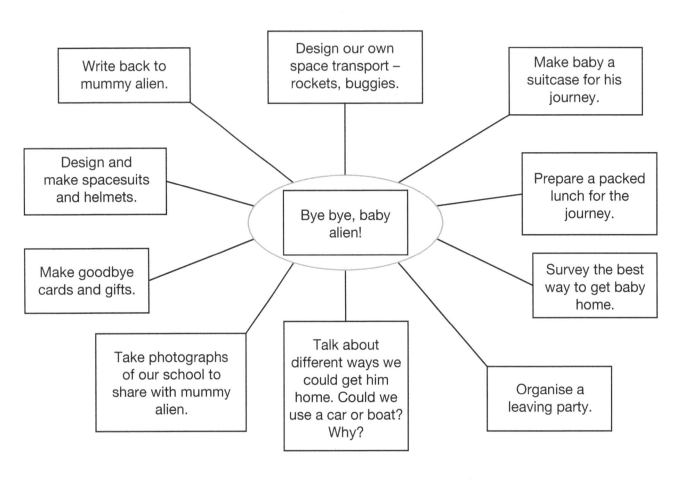

Write back to mummy alien.

Design our own space transport – rockets, buggies.

Make baby a suitcase for his journey.

Design and make spacesuits and helmets.

Bye bye, baby alien!

Prepare a packed lunch for the journey.

Make goodbye cards and gifts.

Survey the best way to get baby home.

Take photographs of our school to share with mummy alien.

Talk about different ways we could get him home. Could we use a car or boat? Why?

Organise a leaving party.

Figure 2.10 *The children made alien models to keep baby alien company on his journey.*

Figure 2.11 *'Alien biscuits' to send with the alien on his journey home.*

SESSION 5: PLANET IGG

The spark!

During the next session, the children receive a photograph of baby alien safely at home with his mummy (see Appendix 2.4). Mummy alien feels that she now knows more about where we live on earth but wants us to discover more about their home in space. Allow the children to talk to their partner about what they already know and what they would like to find out more about. Then gather this in the form of a thought shower (see Appendix 2.5).

What next?

You may like to continue the topic further by investigating more about space. These are the types of activities you may like to include. This is not an exhaustive list, and you may have other ideas that you or the children would like to find out about.

The duration of this topic will depend on the motivation and interest of the children. Use your professional judgement to extend or conclude where appropriate.

PSED

- How would life be different in space?
- Would you like to be an astronaut? Why?
- Would you like to visit space? Why?

Communication and language

- Extend vocabulary to describe space.
- Answer how and why questions on the topic.
- Link topic to previous experiences, such as flying on an aeroplane.
- Make predictions on what life would be like in space.

Physical development

- Travel under and over apparatus linked to a space theme.
- Move space bikes and scooters in and out of obstacles (planets).

- Move in a variety of ways, such as walking in space, taking off like a rocket and walking like an alien.

- Develop fine motor skills – using alien gloop, play dough planets.

- Large-scale messages on the playground to communicate with the astronauts in space.

- Explore foods that astronauts might eat and drink.

Literacy

- Research space using simple books and ICT.

- Read a range of space themed story books.

- Write instructions on how to make a rocket.

- Space and moon poems.

- Write postcards from the moon.

- Make a space menu for an astronaut.

- Describe different planets.

- Label a rocket/astronaut.

Mathematics

- Use positional language to describe the flight of a rocket.

- Compare the weight of 'moon' rocks.

- Count the eyes on different aliens.

- Problem-solve using simple alien word problems.

- Compare and order planets by size.

- Sing space-themed number songs.

- Use space-themed number lines.

- Make rockets from 2D/3D shapes.

- Discuss how long it takes to travel to the moon and relate this to journeys around the school.

Understanding the world

- Investigate real-life astronauts and events – space clips, first man on the moon, first space travel.

- Investigate the solar system.

- Investigate the effects of gravity.

- Look at the sun as a source of light – can we find other sources?

- Could we live on another planet? Why? What do we need to live?

- Use programmable toys on space mats.

- Use computer-based art programs to create space pictures.

- Record messages to and from space using microphones.

Expressive Arts and Design

- Make jetpacks, telescopes, rockets, moon buggies using construction, junk modelling, etc.

- Use bubble painting to create textured planet pictures.

Figure 2.12 A collage 'planet' where baby alien might live.

- Make three-dimensional planets using papier mâché/ModRoc, etc.

- Make play dough/clay aliens.

- Listen to a variety of space-themed music.

- Use instruments to create our own space sounds.

- Show children a picture of space. Discuss the sounds that they might hear. Can they recreate these using their voices, body percussion or instruments, etc.?

Figure 2.13 *A space helmet the children then used in role play.*

- Create our own space dances – a rocket taking off and landing, an astronaut routine, etc.

- Set up your outdoor role play area like a space station.

Continue the project by adding in your own messages from mummy and baby alien. They may like to know how the children are getting on during the project. This is important to continue the children's motivation.

Conclusion

The children may like to share their new-found knowledge of space during a parent sharing afternoon. Here, they become the 'experts' and present what they know to others.

They may like to run a 'space workshop' where they share their work with parents or other members of the school or setting.

Home links

- Look at the types of plants/seeds that we have at home. How are they cared for?

- Find out if any parents or grandparents have their own telescope or an interest in astronomy. They may like to bring this into school or talk to the children.

- Bring in a photograph of their family or home life to share with the alien.

- Ask children to find out about space. Can they find a fabulous fact!

- Encourage the parents to share space-themed stories or information books.

Visits out/visitors in

You may like to visit a museum that has a space exhibition, a local garden centre or botanical gardens, etc.

Investigate whether there are any visitors who could come into school to talk/perform to the children – a local dance or theatre group who could act out a space-themed assembly to evoke the topic.

ENHANCED PROVISION

- Why not try turning your role-play area into a space centre or rocket.
- Add space magazines and space-themed books to your library.
- Display keywords and space-themed vocabulary around your classroom.
- Add glitter and shiny things such as sequins and sea salt to sand, gloop and play dough.
- Transfer the theme outdoors by turning the trikes into space buggies or the climbing frame into a beanstalk.
- Add a planting area complete with seeds and watering cans.
- Use small-world versions of the characters to enhance play and storytelling.
- Add character-themed paper into every area – it is surprising how much incidental writing comes from just this small idea.
- Add small-world spacemen or alien figures to your building area.
- Add posters of popular spacemen and aliens from film and TV.
- Add green gloop, jelly or play dough in the malleable area.
- Turn your water green or add glitter to your water tray. Add in frozen aliens in ice cubes.

My magical seed diary

Name.........

APPENDIX 2.2

The magic seed

'If the sun and rain come, it will grow massive.'
– Ollie

'Eggs are in nests, not in a tree.'
– Fred

'Let's make a ladder and climb up to rescue it.'
– Sandeep

'I would be scared if I was up there.'
– Hetty

'A castle might be at the top, and a giant.'
– Gupreet

'If we keep giving it water, it will grow up to the sky.'
– Alfie

'A caterpillar might have climbed up and laid an egg.'
– Jill

'My mum said if you see eggs in a nest, don't touch them or their mummy might leave them.'
– Sara

'It will be hungry and need a drink.'
– Nathan

'If we are quiet it might peek out and say hello.'
– Livvie

'I think it's a giant flower.'
– Jane

'I think it's on the roof of the school.'
– Bobby

'It's a flower bud, and a daisy might be inside. We can climb up and pick it.'
– Honey

'Put a sign on it saying "don't touch!"'
– Kim

'Why is it in our classroom?'
– Lenny

'It's a baby insect. How many legs has it got?'
– Lilly

'It's a beanstalk like in *Jack and the Beanstalk*'
– Tom

'It might be a sunflower. Mine is as big as that outside.'
– Annabel

'There's an egg on the top and a bird might be inside.'
– Callum

'A flower might be inside. If we water it, it will come out.'
– Harvey

'Don't touch it or it might fall down.'
– Jimmy

'Plant the seeds in the soil and they will grow.'
– Hannah

'If it falls, it might smash, so let's put a net underneath.'
– Polly

the children's ideas when discovering the alien

the children's ideas when discovering the beanstalk

the children's ideas when discovering the egg

APPENDIX 2.3

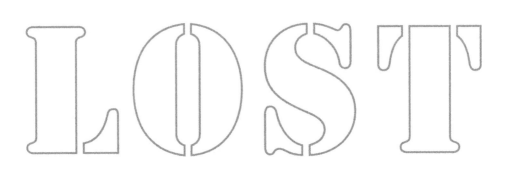

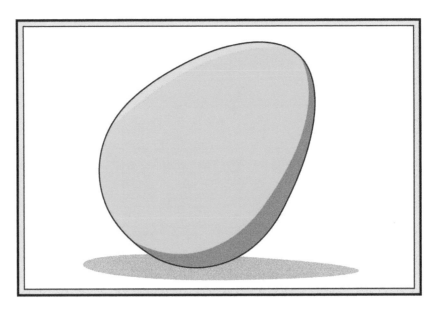

I HAVE LOST MY ALIEN BABY EGG!

IT MAY HAVE LANDED ON EARTH AND

COULD HAVE HATCHED BY NOW.

IF YOU HAVE SEEN IT, PLEASE LET ME KNOW

AND RETURN IT AS SOON AS POSSIBLE.

I AM EXTREMELY UPSET AND WORRIED.

Mummy Alien

154 Space Avenue

Planet Igg

Outer Space

PLANET IGG POST

FIRST CLASS SPACE MAIL

Dear

Thank you so much for looking after my egg and baby. He is now safely back home on Planet Igg. He has learned so much about you earthlings and loved his time with you. I can't thank you enough for taking such good care of him. I now know much more about where you live, but wondered if you knew much about space? Maybe your teacher would help you to find out more? There is so much to investigate.

Lots of love,

Mummy Alien xxx

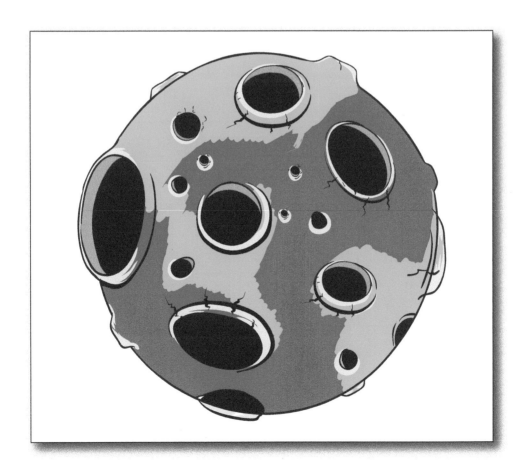

APPENDIX 2.5

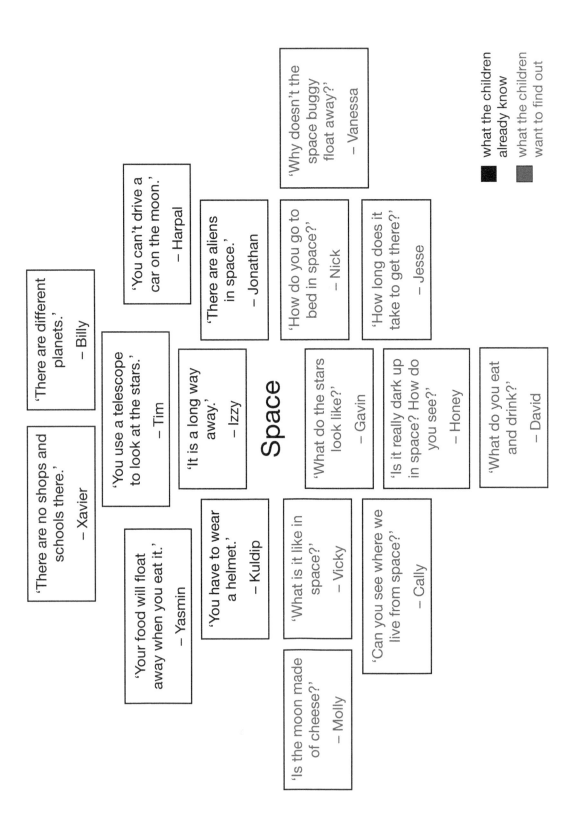

what the children already know

what the children want to find out

Space

'Why doesn't the space buggy float away?' – Vanessa

'You can't drive a car on the moon.' – Harpal

'There are aliens in space.' – Jonathan

'How do you go to bed in space?' – Nick

'How long does it take to get there?' – Jesse

'There are different planets.' – Billy

'You use a telescope to look at the stars.' – Tim

'It is a long way away.' – Izzy

'What do the stars look like?' – Gavin

'Is it really dark up in space? How do you see?' – Honey

'What do you eat and drink?' – David

'There are no shops and schools there.' – Xavier

'Your food will float away when you eat it.' – Yasmin

'You have to wear a helmet.' – Kuldip

'What is it like in space?' – Vicky

'Can you see where we live from space?' – Cally

'Is the moon made of cheese?' – Molly

CHAPTER 3

Nancy the Knight and Lord Lawrence

SETTING THE SCENE

Session 1

The children find a shield, tiara, sword, coins, jewels and horse shoe on the carpet. They discuss who might have visited them and think of ways to keep it safe.

Session 2

Teacher to explain that he/she saw a very strange girl in the playground last night. She was wearing metal clothes and had fallen off a horse. Show the photograph of the girl. Who is she? How can we help her?

Session 3

A golden envelope arrives with a letter from Lord Lawrence. He is glad we have helped his friend, but they now have nowhere to live. Dessie and Daniel, the castle dragons, have been breathing fire and burnt down the castle. Help the children to research castle life and design.

Session 4

Now the children are more knowledgeable about castles, they can proceed to design and make their own castles for Nancy and Lawrence.

Session 5

Set up a glittery dragon-shaped footprint and scroll message from Nancy. The dragons have escaped from dragon school and are refusing to go back. Nancy is worried they will burn down the newly built castle. The children help to teach the mischievous dragons how to behave appropriately.

Session 6 and beyond

Peace is restored to the castle and the dragons have attended school again. To celebrate, Nancy and Lawrence would like the children's help to hold a royal banquet.

SESSION 1: STARTING POINTS

The spark!

When the children arrive in the classroom, they discover a strange set of objects have been left behind. The children then discuss who they might belong to and why they are there. We used items shown in the photograph. These were quite open-ended and perfect for discussion.

Figure 3.1 *Examples of items you may want the children to discover.*

What can we do to help?

- Make 'found' posters to display around the school clearly showing the items in case the owners come looking for them.

- Create a video message or small news report that could be shown to other classes in school, explaining what has happened and requesting further help.

- Draw or paint who they think the items might belong to.

- Create and record their own questions. For example: Who left these items? What were you doing in our classroom? Why did you leave them behind?

This session provides a great opportunity for the adult to create a thought shower that will help inform future planning. You may like to record ideas they have about the items in one colour and ideas to help in another.

REMEMBER

Be flexible . . . allow the children to lead the discussion. Be aware of their abilities and scaffold their thinking if needed. The children may decide on different ideas to those suggested . . . go with them.

SESSION 2: SPECIAL VISITOR

The spark!

For this session, gather the children together and recap on what you found yesterday. While this is happening, you or another member of staff can explain the imaginary scene you witnessed last night (based on the script from Appendix 3.1). Explain that you took a photograph that you would like to share with the children. Show the picture of Nancy the Knight (see Appendix 3.2) and explain that this is the person you saw in the playground.

Be convincing!

Remember to use your best acting skills as you deliver the script. It will work best if you use the script as a basis to share your encounter rather than reading it word for word. The children will engage more and the scenario will become more believable the more effort you put into this dilemma.

Be creative!

You may even like to ask your head teacher or caretaker to come and share the news with the children. You can then act as shocked as they will be! The more dramatic this session is, the better.

And next . . .

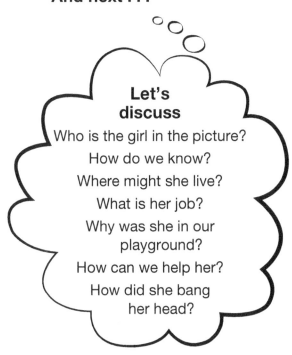

Let's discuss

Who is the girl in the picture?

How do we know?

Where might she live?

What is her job?

Why was she in our playground?

How can we help her?

How did she bang her head?

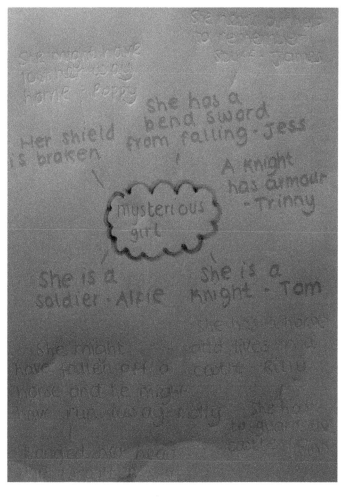

Figure 3.2 *These are the types of thoughts that the children generated.*

HOW CAN WE HELP?

Remember, it is important to let the children help you plan, so use their ideas too. These are just some examples that you might like to incorporate or use if your children need more ideas.

Discuss what a knight is and what we already know about knights.

Write rules about how to be a good knight for Nancy to follow.

Make Nancy some new armour.

Introduce the idea of a family coat of arms and encourage children to design their own. The children may like to put this on to a new shield for Nancy.

Create 'get well soon' cards for Nancy.

Make lists of what a knight needs.

As Nancy has lost her horse, make new ways for her to travel.

Research knights and their roles using class library and Internet.

Draw and paint what a knight should look like.

Put posters up around school to see if anyone recognises Nancy.

Figure 3.3 *The children may make their own armour and shields.*

Figure 3.4 *Examples of the types of cards the children might make.*

SESSION 3: DESSIE AND DANIEL

The spark!

A letter arrives in the classroom in a golden envelope. Begin the session by sharing this with the children (see Appendix 3.3). Discuss the letter from Lord Lawrence and the problem he now faces. This session depends on the children's prior knowledge. If they have limited knowledge about what a castle is and its features, you may like to take the time to research this further using a range of sources.

★ Find out what the children already know about castles and the people who live there.

★ Use non-fiction books, ICT or even a child expert in your class to find out more about castles.

★ This is a great starting point for your planning. Depending on the knowledge of the children, this session may simply be a research session.

What do we need to learn . . .

> • What is a castle?
>
> • What is inside a castle?
>
> • Why were they built?
>
> • What jobs take place inside?
>
> • What features do castles have?
>
> • Who works in/outside the castle?
>
> • Who lives in the castle?
>
> • How are castles different to our homes today?
>
> • How do castles protect the people who live inside them?

Home links

• This is a great opportunity to ask the children to find out an interesting fact about castles at home.

• Have any children ever visited a castle in their local area?

SESSION 4: A NEW HOME

Once the children are more familiar with castle life and design, they are now more equipped to help Nancy the Knight and Lord Lawrence design and make their new home.

Begin by asking the children what a castle needs. (This becomes the 'success criteria' that must be included in designs. Children can then evaluate their design against this at the end of the session.)

See our example. Your children may suggest other things they feel are important.

A castle needs . . .

► A secure door
► To be high on a hill
► To be in a safe place
► To have turrets
► To have small arrow slit windows
► To have strong walls
► To have a flag

Try to pair the children into small groups so they can work together to design a new class castle. Here, the children designed large-scale designs that they later shared with the class. The success criteria helped to scaffold their designs and promote self-evaluation: 'We had a strong door but forgot the small windows.'

From these designs, the children can then make their own castles from a range of suitable materials.

Figure 3.5 *A design produced by one of the children.*

★ Construction, such as blocks and bricks. This can be done indoors or outdoors.
★ Junk modelling using boxes, pots and rolls.
★ Papier mâché or Modroc.
★ Large boxes, pallets or planks. These are particularly useful for outdoor use.
★ Use den-making kits, blankets, pegs or tents.

Bringing the castle alive in your classroom

Try asking the children to help you set up a castle in your role-play area for Nancy and Lawrence to live in. They will love having the responsibility and ownership of creating their own special creative role-play area. This will help promote creative play and bring the whole topic to life.

Why not try . . .

- Write shopping lists of things we need for our castle.
- Write to your head teacher to ask if we can set up a castle in school.
- Raise money through a cake sale, craft sale, etc. to buy items we may need, such as props and costumes.
- Print or collage the walls of the castle.
- Create labels for the role-play area, such as arrow slits, portcullis and turrets.
- Make tidy up time rules or add photographs of how the castle should look at the end of the day.
- Make the portcullis using different textured materials.
- Make a list of castle jobs that need to be carried out each day.
- Make flags and shields for the castle interior.
- Make crown, swords, arrows and tiaras for the role play.

Figure 3.6 The children can then use their castle for role play.

Remember to add in castle-themed writing paper, numbers and letters, castle books and props to help inspire all areas of learning.

Figure 3.7 The children created their own flags and coat of arms.

Figure 3.8 The children made their own armour and helmets to use in their role play.

SESSION 5: MISCHIEVOUS DRAGONS

The spark!

Setting up . . . make a glittery dragon-shaped footprint on the carpet or classroom table. This could be done with glitter, green powder paint, etc. On the floor or table, add a pile of books, toys and crumpled-up paper. Next to the footprint, place a scroll with the message from Nancy (see Appendix 3.4).

The castle dragons have escaped from dragon school and are being very mischievous. They need to return immediately!

Figure 3.9 *Mysterious footprints.*

Time to talk . . .

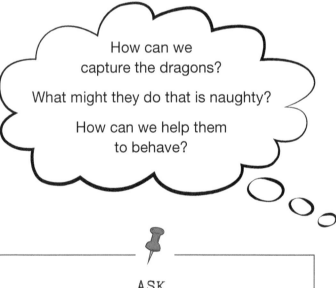

How can we capture the dragons?

What might they do that is naughty?

How can we help them to behave?

ASK

- Have the children heard of any famous dragons?

- Share dragon stories during group time.

POSSIBLE ACTIVITIES

Literacy

- Write to Lord Lawrence saying we will help.
- Write dragon rules to remind them to behave.
- Make signs to keep the dragons out of the classroom.

Understanding the world

- Make maps to help look for the dragons.
- Find out more about fire safety and explain the dangers of breathing fire to the dragons.
- Create voice messages to the dragons using video cameras, microphones, etc.

Expressive Arts and Design

- Make dragon traps.
- Make dragon masks to help secretly search for the dragons.
- Create dragon dances.
- Create dragon music.
- Design and make dragon food.
- Large-scale textured dragons.
- Make dragon caves.

PSED

- Why do we have rules?
- How did we feel when the dragons messed up our classroom?
- Why do they need to go to school?
- Have we ever done things that we shouldn't?
- Create rewards for if the dragons behave . . . star chart, stickers, medals.

Mathematics

- Use positional language to describe where the dragons are hiding.
- Dragon word problems: Four dragons hide and one runs away. How many are left?

Physical development

- This runs throughout as the children develop their fine motor control through cutting, pencil holding, etc.
- Large-scale maps can be drawn outdoors.
- Obstacle courses can be set up outdoors – stepping stones through the swamp, over the plank bridge, through the climbing frame forest.

Figure 3.10 *Making dragon caves to help capture the dragons.*

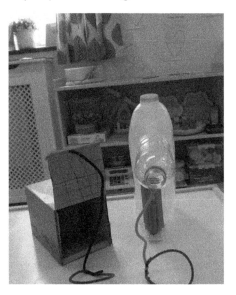

Figure 3.11 *Dragon traps: 'Let's put food inside and they will eat it and get captured.'*

SESSION 6: THE ROYAL BANQUET

Synopsis

Peace is restored to the castle. The dragons have decided to return to school. To celebrate, Nancy and Lawrence would like to hold a royal banquet.

Following the script from Appendix 3.5, you may like to record this in the form of a voice message from Lord Lawrence or Nancy the Knight. Lord Lawrence and Nancy the Knight are hoping to attend the special celebration to say thank you for all of our help. This can be done on a smartphone. Play the message to the children and ask if they can help prepare the classroom for the celebratory banquet. These are the types of activities that can be continued until the day of the planned banquet. This may last for several days or even weeks, depending on the level of engagement. Parents can be invited to attend and the children can dress up as their chosen character. This is a real climax to the whole project. It is a culmination of the children's knowledge and a celebration of their hard work, so make it as exciting as you can!

HOW CAN WE HELP?

PSED

- Look at teamwork. How can we organise the banquet together?

Literacy

- Write to head teacher to ask permission.

- Plan what we need to prepare.

- Write lists of what we need to make/buy.

- Make banquet menus.

- Make posters to advertise the banquet.

- Send invites to parents we would like to invite.

Figure 3.12 *Designing menus.*

Mathematics

- Compile a class survey of favourite castle characters/food to eat at the banquet.

- Weigh out quantities of food when preparing the banquet.

- Solve simple problems. For example: We have six guests and 12 cakes. How can we divide the cakes between them? There are five knights on one table. How many knights on two tables?

Understanding the world

- Look at the roles of different people within the castle and discuss who we would like to be on the day of the banquet.

- Record advertisements for the banquet using video cameras/microphones.

- Design posters using ICT programs.

Expressive Arts and Design

Figure 3.13 *Costumes to wear on the day.*

- Design costumes to wear.
- Create castle decorations (e.g. bunting, flags, place mats).
- Perform medieval dances.
- Listen to medieval music and make their own.

Day of the banquet

Ask an important member of staff in your setting, such as the school secretary or head teacher, to announce that, unfortunately, Lord Lawrence and Nancy the Knight are unable to attend due to royal commitments. They have sent something special for the children and wondered if they could take good care of it until they can visit another time. The special adult presents the box of treasures. (This can be a box of jewellery, gems, coins and other sparkly treasures.) Decide together where you are going to keep the box of treasure so that it is safe.

Figure 3.14 *A castle made by one of the children.*

ENHANCED PROVISION

- Add castle-themed books and stories to your classroom.
- Display keywords and character names around your classroom.
- Transfer the theme outdoors by adding large-scale construction, which can be used to build castles and fortresses.
- Use small-world castles and dragons to enhance play and storytelling.
- Add castle-themed paper into every area.
- Add crowns, shields and tiaras into your classroom.
- Use castle stickers in your creative/making area.
- Use popular culture castle and knight characters, which the children may see on television, in your classroom.

Sharing our knowledge

The whole topic provides scope to be shared during a special class assembly. The children can share the story of Nancy and Lawrence, their ideas and creations, as well as their newly gained castle knowledge. They can perform their special dances and learn castle-themed songs to sing.

APPENDIX 3.1

Well, you will never guess what happened to me after school last night. As I was tidying the classroom, I heard an almighty bump, crash, bang, wallop in the playground. So I ran outside to see what was going on! There in the middle of the playground was a black horse galloping around in and out of the fences, eating all of the grass. What on earth was a horse doing in our playground?

As I ran over to catch it, I saw a strange sight sitting on the floor in a heap. It was a little girl but she wasn't in uniform. She was wearing a hard silver costume, boots and a helmet. I think she said it was called armour, but as she had bumped her head she couldn't remember who she was and what she was doing. I helped her up and brought her into school. All of her armour was broken, her sword had snapped and her shield was cracked.

She just couldn't remember a thing and was very confused. I took her to the head teacher's office, who took her to the hospital immediately.

I promised that we would help her to remember. I thought maybe you would know why she was wearing these strange clothes and riding a horse? Maybe you know what her job is and where she might live? And of course, her horse has disappeared, so she really needs our help! Whatever are we going to do?

APPENDIX 3.2

APPENDIX 3.3

Dear children,

Let me take the time to introduce myself. My name is Lord Lawrence and I hear that you have been helping my friend, Nancy the Knight, after her fall from Hetty, her horse. Thank you so much for helping her to remember her knightly duties. She absolutely adores the things you have made for her. You are all extremely kind children.

Unfortunately, our castle dragons, Daniel and Dessie, have been rather silly, and while they were breathing fire they mistakenly burned our castle down! It is nothing more than a pile of ash and smoke! This is awfully bad news and now we are homeless.

I really hope you all know about castles and can help us to build a new one? It isn't like a normal house, you know. It needs to keep us safe and protected.

I look forward to hearing from you all and sincerely hope you can help.

Kind regards,
Lord Lawrence and Nancy the Knight xx

APPENDIX 3.4

Help!

It's Nancy the Knight here! Thank you for our beautiful new castle. It is just perfect.

Just one problem – Daniel and Dessie the dragons are causing trouble again! This time, they have escaped from dragon school and are being very naughty.

They are refusing to go to school and I am worried they will burn the castle down again. We can't find them anywhere! Please help. They must learn how to behave.

Love from,
Nancy xx

Wow-ee, it's Nancy and Lord Lawrence calling to say thank you for all of your wonderful help. We have managed to use (insert child's name and idea) to capture Daniel and Dessie the dragons. They have read through all of the dragon rules you told them and understand that they have been extremely naughty lately. They understand that it is very dangerous to breathe fire inside the castle and would like to say sorry to everyone for all of the trouble they have caused. Like you (or an individual child's name) told them, school is important to help them learn, and so they are happy to start back today.

We are so happy that peace has been restored to our castle, and to thank you we would like to hold a grand banquet at your school. We are sure that you can find out everything that a banquet needs as you are all so very clever. With the help of your teacher, (insert name), you can plan and make everything you need.

This will be a right royal celebration, and the perfect way to say thank you for all of your hard work.

We look forward to hearing from you soon. God luck with the banquet planning. You have lots to do, so get busy!

Best royal wishes,
　　　　　Nancy the Knight and Lord Lawrence xx

CHAPTER 4

A pirate adventure

SETTING THE SCENE

Session 1

The children are now looking after Nancy and Lawrence's jewels. They enter the room one morning to discover they are gone, and in their place are a few feathers, dropped gems and twigs. On exploring the scene, they find a scroll from Captain Finne explaining that his boat has been shipwrecked. He sent his parrot, Piper, who took the jewels thinking she could use them to purchase a new ship. Captain Finne needs our help to fix the ship and find Piper. As soon as Piper is found, the jewels will be returned.

Session 2

A message in a bottle arrives stating that Captain Finne has sent the children a shipbuilding challenge.

Session 3

Captain Finne is delighted with the boats the children have made. Unfortunately, he has lost all of his pirate belongings in the flood. What does he need? How can we help?

Session 4

Now the captain has been helped by the children, he is back on the sea and looking for Piper. Can the children help him?

Session 5

The treasure is returned to the classroom, as well as a message from Piper. She is extremely sorry for the problems she has caused and will never behave in such a way again.

SESSION 1: STARTING POINTS

The spark!

The children are now looking after the jewels and treasures for Lord Lawrence and Nancy the Knight. As they enter the room one morning, they will notice that they have disappeared. On the carpet nearby, you can add in clues such as brightly coloured feathers, dropped jewels, seed and a few twigs.

Time to think . . .

Figure 4.1 *These are the items we used to ignite the excitement and curiosity.*

Who has been in our classroom?

What clues do we have?

Why have they taken our treasure?

Where might it be?

How can we get it back?

SETTING THE SCENE

This is a short discussion where the children generate ideas on what may have happened and why. It leads quickly into the next clue being found.

What next . . . ?

As you investigate the missing items further, add in a scroll or message. This could be inside the empty treasure chest or high up on the window. This is from Captain Finne sending his apologies. His not-so-clever parrot, Piper, was sent for help after they became shipwrecked. On finding the classroom empty, she thought the treasure could be used to help purchase a new ship for the crew. However, she became lost on her return to the ship. How can the children help? Once Captain Finne can set sail again, he can return the treasure (see Appendix 4.1).

Let's talk . . .

First, gather the children together; you may like to use 'talk partners' to discuss what we know about pirates and how they think we can help the captain. Remember to discuss the key points:

- What is a pirate?

- What is their role?

- What do they do?

- What do they wear?

- What do they need?

- What does 'shipwrecked' mean?

- How can we help them?

- What is special about a pirate ship? How is it different from other ships?

Keeping your evidence

Initially, record the children's knowledge at the beginning of the project. Add in what they would like to find out and any questions they wish to ask. Develop this further by jotting on their suggestions for ways they can help Captain Finne (these form your activities for each session).

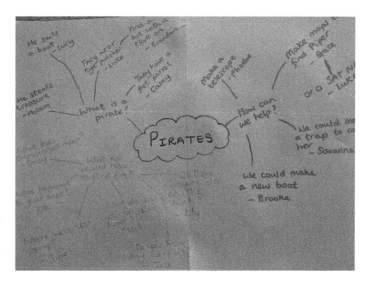

This is a great way to record your project as it develops. On the conclusion of the topic, you can add in the things the children now know.

Figure 4.2 Add in details as the topic progresses.

Let's help

Create a class letter (or individual letters if your children are able) of reply to the pirate. Encourage or model how to compose the letter. Remind the children that they are explaining that they would like to help and ways that they plan to do this.

The children may like to record what they know about pirates to share during the session. This could include creating pictures, drawings, paintings, models, jottings and writing.

SESSION 2: THE CHALLENGE

A message in a bottle arrives to say that Captain Finne is pleased that we can help. He has sent us our first challenge. Read the challenge together and generate ideas on how we can complete it successfully (see Appendix 4.2).

And then . . .

 Children discuss what a boat needs.

Children design their own boat.

 Children test out suitable materials they can use to construct it.

Children explore floating and sinking.

Children make their boat.

Children test out if their boat meets Captain Finne's wishes.

Children evaluate what was successful and what they would change.

Figure 4.3 *A boat created for the pirate challenge.*

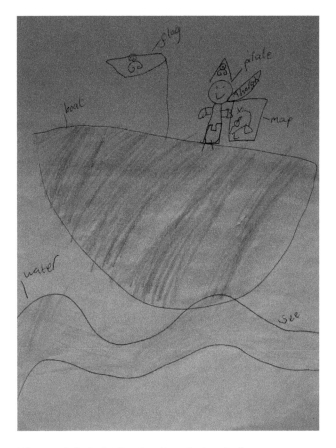

Figure 4.4 *A design for the pirate challenge.*

Further development

You may like to develop your class role-play area into a pirate ship. The children can use their ship designs to help you. As the project develops, they can add in other pirate-themed items that they make.

Remember, child-led role play promotes a sense of ownership. The children are more likely to respect a role-play area they have created themselves, and therefore use it purposefully.

SESSION 3: SHIPWRECK

The spark!

Captain Finne is delighted with the new boats. Use the script to explain his next dilemma (see Appendix 4.3). You may like to use a smartphone to record a message from him (in your best pirate voice!) or class telephone where you 'call him' in front of the children and feed back to them immediately.

The dilemma

All of the pirates' belongings were washed away during the shipwreck, and so the crew cannot set sail to find Piper.

Provoking thought

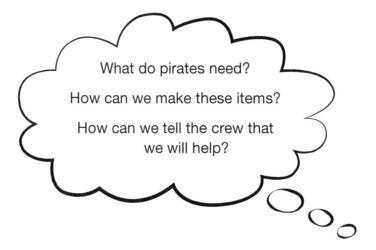

What do pirates need?

How can we make these items?

How can we tell the crew that we will help?

★   Use the children's knowledge, as well as pirate-themed books, prepared
    ICT presentations, Internet and home learning, to find out more.

HOW CAN WE HELP?

Physical development

- Develop large-scale apparatus to act out a pirate-themed play. 'Walk the plank', 'Climb the mast', etc.

- Use large- and small-scale construction to create pirate ships, swords, treasure chests, etc.

Figure 4.5 *The children created a large pirate ship to use in their play.*

Literacy

- Write messages to the captain.

- Make list of the items a pirate needs.

- Label pirate costume designs.

- Research pirate theme using class library/Internet.

- Make rules to help the new ship to sail smoothly.

- Label the role-play area.

- Read stories about famous pirates.

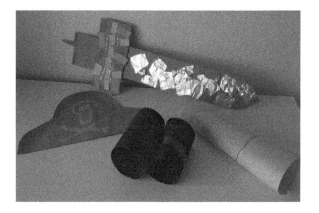

Figure 4.6 *The children made their own role-play items.*

Understanding the world

- Discuss where pirates are found.

- Talk about sea travel and look at the world globe to identify sea and land.

- Use programmable toys to navigate a route on the seas.

- Use laptops and PCs to find out more. This could be given as a family project to promote home-school links.

- Add various materials into your water tray to test out floating and sinking.

Expressive Arts and Design

- Create a class pirate ship.

- Design and create their own costumes for the pirates.

- Design a new flag.

- Make eyepatches.

- Make pirate hats.

- Design treasure chests for the stolen treasure.

PSNR

- Use the language of measure to compare capacities. Add various-sized containers into your water tray.

- Solve pirate-themed number problems. For example: There are two pirates on the plank, and three more are added. How many pirates are on the plank altogether?

Figure 4.7 *A labelled drawing of Captain Finne.*

SESSION 4: FINDING PIPER

The spark!

A postcard arrives from the captain. He is now on his new boat and kitted out as a pirate again. He needs our help to track down Piper the parrot and explain to her that she must return our class treasure (see Appendix 4.4). Gather the children together to discuss the problem. How can we find Piper? What are we going to do to help?

How can we help?

This then leads to a wealth of activities that the children can decide upon to help find Piper. Below are some examples you may wish to use.

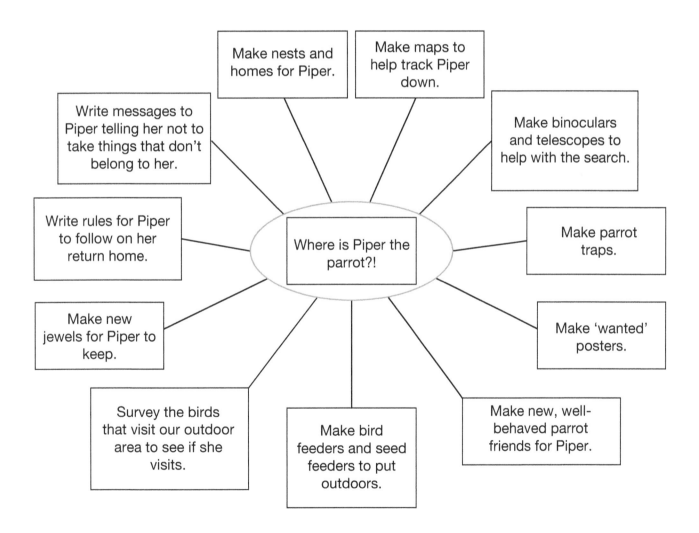

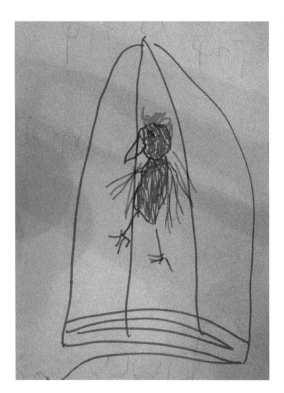

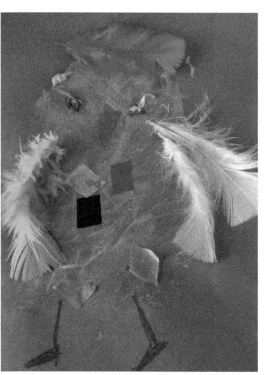

Figure 4.8 *'I'm going to catch Piper in a bird cage.'*

Figure 4.9 *The children made posters to help find Piper.*

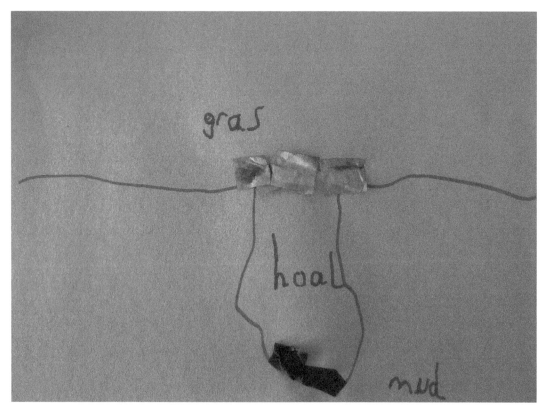

Figure 4.10 *One of the children designed a trap to catch Piper.*

SESSION 5: THE TREASURE

Concluding the project

The treasure is returned to the classroom along with a thank you note from Piper the parrot. She knows that what she did was wrong and wants to apologise. Be imaginative in your delivery. We have previously used a parrot hand puppet to deliver this message. The children have loved having Piper visit them, and this acts as a great concluding session (see Appendix 4.4).

Home links

- Can the children find out a fabulous pirate fact?

- Parents may like to help out by sending in items that can be used for building the pirate ships.

- There are lots of pirate-themed television programmes that can be watched together at home.

- You may like to learn pirate-themed songs or sea shanties that can be sent home to be practised together.

- Send home a special 'treasure bag' that the children can fill with their own treasure. These are items that are special to them.

Figure 4.11 *Jewellery made for Piper to keep.*

Figure 4.12 *You may like to enhance your provision by adding jewels to the sand and water play.*

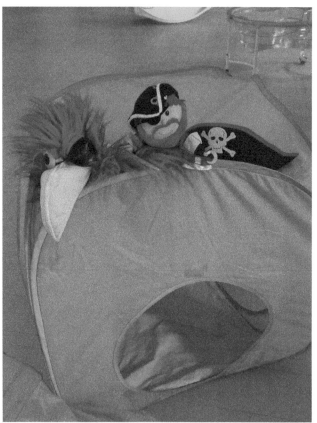

Figure 4.13 *Add puppets and costumes to your role play.*

ENHANCED PROVISION

- Your outdoor area can be changed into a pirate delight, complete with sand tray beach and paddling pool sea.
- Ask the children to bring in pirate-themed books to share.
- Display keywords and pirate-themed vocabulary around your classroom.
- Add seashells into your printing area, sand and water trays.
- Transfer the theme outdoors by adding costumes into your areas.
- Use small-world versions of the characters to enhance play and storytelling.
- Add sand and water into your construction area.
- Add maps and telescopes around the room.
- Hold a pirate dressing up day to promote imaginative play.

APPENDIX 4.1

Yo-ho-ho, me hearties,

Terrible news I send ye . . . my ship has become shipwrecked on some rocks and I sent my not-so-clever parrot, Piper, for help!

On flying into your classroom, she foolishly saw your treasure and took it with her. When she returned here, she said we could sell it to buy a new ship.

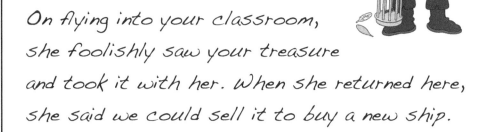

I explained that 'tis stealing and that she must return it to ye immediately! The daft parrot was flying to give it back and got lost on the way!

I must find her, repair my boat and set sail to return your precious cargo! Can ye help me?

Captain Finne xx

APPENDIX 4.2

Yo-ho-ho, me hearties,

Thanks so much for agreeing to help me. I was really worried that I would never be able to set sail again and find Piper the parrot. I need a new pirate ship, but it needs several things to make it into a proper boat suitable for my crew:

1 It must float for at least 30 seconds.

2 It must hold two pirates.

3 It must have a sail.

I look forward to seeing your new boats really soon. Your teacher will send the winning boat to me so I can begin my journey.

Shiver me timbers,

Captain Finne

APPENDIX 4.3

Hey, me hearties,

'Tis Captain Finne here. I am delighted with ye hard work and help. Ye teacher, _ _ _ _ _ _ _ _ _ _ _ (INSERT NAME), has said how hard ye all have been working for me.

(YOU CAN ADD IN CHILDREN'S NAMES AND WHAT THEY MADE TO BRING THIS TO LIFE.)

I love the boats and ships ye have designed and made for me. They be perfect for a pirate like me and my crew. I especially liked

(AGAIN, MENTION FEATURES FROM CHILDREN'S DESIGNS.)

'Tis so good to be back on the sea. As our old ship was so damaged by the sea, all of our pirate clothes and belongings have been washed away. We have nothing left!

Do ye think you can help out again?

APPENDIX 4.4

Land ahoy, me hearties,

Captain Finne here! Finally set sail on
the new pirate ship you designed and made for
me. I have my new pirate costume and hat on
and feel like a proper pirate again! We still have
a dilemma ... Piper is still missing, and ye must
help me to track her down. I want her to give
ye your treasure back. Let's find her together.
Captain Finne xx

APPENDIX 4.5

Dear pirate kids,

Thank you for helping my master, Captain Finne, to set sail and find me. I am so sorry for taking your treasure.

I only did it to help Captain Finne and my shipmates but I now realise how silly I've been.

Us parrots can be a bit silly sometimes but I won't ever do it again!

You have been so very kind. We will never forget what you have done . . . you are all honorary pirates.

Love Piper x

CHAPTER 5

PC Pete and Detective Della

SETTING THE SCENE

Session 1

Find a police badge, keys, dog toy and letter from Detective Della explaining that PC Pete has broken down and his sniffer dog, Donny, has escaped. Can we help?

Session 2

Paint paw prints on a table and add in a dog tag and collar. As the children find the clues, discuss who they belong to. A little later, place a dog puppet in the playground (in a tree or climbing frame). A member of staff hears scratching or barking and leads the children to the discovery of Donny. How can we get him down safely?

Session 3

Donny is now in the classroom thanks to the children's ideas. The children must care for him and safely return him to PC Pete.

Session 4 (optional)

As the children enjoyed looking after Donny the dog so much, you and your head teacher thought it would be good for the children to have a class pet. Set up an exploratory session where the children can research different pets in order to find the best one to have in the classroom. Explore the possibilities and find out what you will need to take care of the class pet you choose.

Session 5

Detective Della wanted to thank the children for their help. She went to the post office to post a thank you card, and when she arrived the wind had blown a tree down that had broken the window of the post office. Everything inside had blown away. The post office had been destroyed. Can the children create a new one?

Session 6

An email arrives from PC Pete explaining that the local firefighters have all come down with chickenpox, so unfortunately Safetown fire station has had to be closed. Do the children know anything about firefighters? Can they help?

And beyond . . .

You may like to explore other scenarios linked to other people who may live in safetown (e.g. doctor, dentist, mechanic, etc.).

Setting the scene

- Prior to the topic, you may like to talk to the children about their knowledge of the police force. Do they know their role and the jobs they undertake? Have they ever had any experience of the police helping them or their family?

- You may like to arrange a visit to a local police station.

- You could invite your local PCO into your setting. The children can ask them questions to find out more about their role.

- Add simple factual books and stories about the police force into your daily story time sessions.

SESSION 1: STARTING POINTS

```
RESOURCES NEEDED

• PC Pete's identity badge
  (see Appendix 5.1)

• car keys

• a dog toy or dog treat

• letter from Detective Della
  (see Appendix 5.2)
```

Figure 5.1 *These are the items the children found when they entered our setting.*

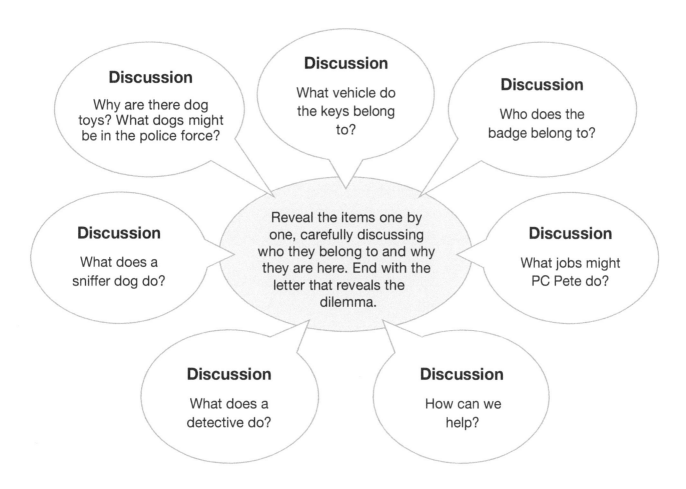

Planning with the children

Develop the discussion into planning ways that they can help to solve the dilemma. There are two problems that need our attention. You may like to use talk partners to allow the children time to generate activity ideas.

1 Donny the dog is missing.

2 PC Pete's police van has broken down so he can't continue with his job.

Create a list with the children. Record their ideas about what they are going to do to help. Remember, these are suggestions; your children may have many more of their own. The next page provides a list of some possible activities that could be provided on day 1 of the topic.

HOW CAN WE HELP?

Expressive Arts and Design

Use construction/junk modelling/chosen materials to make a new police vehicle.

Expressive Arts and Design/moving and handling focus

Make tools to help fix the broken-down van.

Figure 5.2 *Tools to help fix the van.*

Writing focus

Write to Detective Daisy agreeing to help.

Understanding the world/Expressive Arts and Design/writing

Draw maps of the local area to send to PC Pete to help with the search.

Reading/Expressive Arts and Design/ understanding the world

Look at car magazines to help design new police cars/vans.

Figure 5.3 *Enhanced small-world play.*

Expressive Arts and Design/moving and handling focus

Make items to help with the search – telescopes, nets, traps, helicopters, etc.

Mathematics/understanding the world/Expressive Arts and Design

Investigate padlocks and design and make new ones for Pete to use.

Expressive Arts and Design/moving and handling focus

Make new safety crates for Donny the dog on his return.

Technology/writing/moving and handling focus

Use simple drawing programs to create 'missing' posters/advertisements.

Technology/speaking focus

Record police announcements about Donny the dog. Focus on the language they use.

> **Why not . . .**
> Add plastic tools or a mechanic role play into your outdoor area. The children can help fix their vehicles or turn the bikes into police cars.

SESSION 2: MISSING DOG

The spark!

Getting ready . . .

Paint paw prints on the table or use powder paint to create muddy-looking paw prints. Add in a real dog tag or laminated version (see Appendix 5.3). You will need a small dog teddy that you will need to hide somewhere in the classroom or outdoor area. It works best in quite a high place such as a tree or climbing frame.

Awe and wonder . . .

As the children enter the classroom, they will hopefully notice the prints and tag! This will lead to the next series of events.

Figure 5.4 Donny the dog trapped in our outdoor area.

What a surprise that these items are in our classroom . . .

Who do they belong to? Who has been here? Is he still here? Where might he be? How did he get here? How might he be feeling?

The children should link these to yesterday's problem and see that Donny might be hiding somewhere in our room. Depending on the experience of the children, you may need to remind and scaffold this initially.

And then . . .

During this discussion, send a member of staff and a few children on an errand. Ensure that they walk past the area where you have hidden Donny. Prompt the adult to draw the children's attention to this (if not spotted already).

'I'm sure I can hear scratching up that tree . . . oh my goodness, what's that?'

Let your imagination run wild here! Suspend your disbelief.

'We better go and tell the other children to come and look!'

Figure 5.5 We can make a ladder to help him climb down.

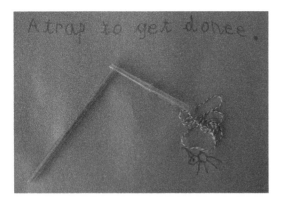

Figure 5.6 *'Put in some bones and he will climb down.'*

So Donny has been discovered but needs the children's help to get him down safely. The children will hopefully generate multiple ways of helping him. Remember to provide lots of open-ended resources to allow them to explore and investigate these ideas. These ideas may include parachutes, ladders, slides, jetpacks, helicopters, rockets, messages of support for Donny, and so on.

SESSION 3: SAFE AND SOUND

The wow factor!

Place Donny the dog in your classroom. Explain to the children that after school/nursery, you used some of their ideas to rescue him (you may like to specifically pick one of the children's creations to refer to). He is safe and well but you have no idea how to take care of him or how to return him to PC Pete.

Create a thought shower of what the children know about how to care for a dog like Donny. Do they have dogs as pets? What do they need to be safe and healthy? Try to incorporate their own first-hand experiences.

'My dog needs lots of walks.' – Molly
'Yes, but he might run away again.' – Tom
'Not if you put him on a lead.' – Molly

'He will need a nice soft bed to sleep in, or a basket.' – Joshua

'My dog has his name tag on.' – Billy
'What is on the tag?' – Mrs G
'Well, his name and where he lives.' – Billy
'And your phone number.' – Jessica

'PC Pete will be happy to see Donny. Let's call him and tell him!' – Jimmy
'We could write to him too.' – Rani

'I think Donny will be hungry and need a drink because he was stuck up the tree. I'm going to get him some water and bones.' – Savanna
'And some dog food and biscuits.' – Mina
'Donny might try to run away again. I'm going to tell him not to so he knows how to be a good dog.' – Sonny

'Donny might need some toys to play with, but not toys like we have.' – Harpreet
'What kind of toys?' – Mr H
'Balls, bones or a squeaky toy like a rabbit.' – Harpreet

During your discussion, encourage children to independently choose how to make their creations. Careful intervention can help to prompt and guide thinking. Promote reflective thinking and self-evaluation as you work alongside the children.

Use questions such as:

- How are you going to make that?

- Is that the best choice? Why?

- What do you need to include?

- What was really good about your . . . ?

- What would you change to make it better?

You may like to include success steps to guide the thinking process:

- I can draw and cut out my tag.

- I can write on his name.

- I can write on his telephone number.

- I can attach it safely to his collar.

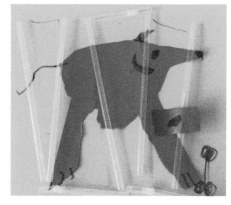

Figure 5.7 *A crate to prevent Donny running away again.*

Figure 5.8 *Collars for Donny to wear.*

Conclusion

Gather the children together and share their creations. Pick a selection of work for Donny to take with him on his journey home. You may like to set the children some success criteria in order to help you narrow down the pieces you choose. Explain that at the end of the day, you will be returning Donny to PC Pete along with their creations.

Figure 5.9 *'My dog goes in a special cage in our car.'*

SESSION 4: CLASS PET

The spark!

Explain that as the children enjoyed looking after Donny the dog, you and PC Pete thought the children would like a class pet to care for.

Initial thoughts

Complete a simple survey such as the one below.

Would a dog like Donny be a good class pet?	
Yes	**No**
'He is a friendly Dog.' – Jane	'He has nowhere to sleep.' – Tom
'He loves the boys and girls.' – Harry	'He needs lots of walks and we are busy in class.' – Amy
	'He is too big.' – Kally
	'He barks a lot and the head teacher might not like it.' – Fred
	'He likes to play and we are doing work.' – Nina
	'What about weekends?' – Gavin

What would be a better pet for school and why? Let's explore . . .

- Discuss the pets the children have at home. Are these more suitable? Why?
- Survey our favourite pets. Create a tally chart and simple pictogram.
- Arrange a visit from an animal roadshow or workshop to find out more about pets' needs.
- Research our favourite pets and their needs.
- Make homes for the pets we choose.
- Create a class pet shop or vets role-play area.
- Create simple fact files and pet care sheets to send to PC Pete to help with his choice.
- Draw/paint/collage/make models of our favourite pets.
- Write back to PC Pete explaining their choices.

Discuss how having a pet at home is different to a class pet. There are lots of speaking and listening skills here – even the first steps of debating.

This may lead to you purchasing your own class pet. Home links can be made here as the children could take it home to care for over the weekend.

Figure 5.10 *'A hamster is small and quiet for the classroom.'*

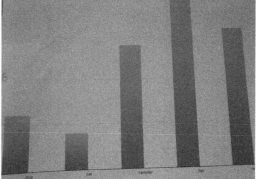

Figure 5.11 *'A sausage dog is small and a good pet.'*

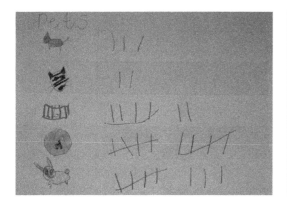

Figure 5.12 One child asked her friends which pets they preferred.

Figure 5.13 We worked together to produce a bar chart.

Depending on the children's interest in this topic, it may last several days or weeks. You may like to move on to look at the role of the vet and even arrange a visit to a veterinary surgery. If you are based in a more rural area, you could extend by exploring different types of farm animals. You could compare these with more domestic pets. The topic of animals could be extended in many ways. Just remember to be creative and go along with the children's ideas and interests.

Conclusion

Ask your head teacher or setting manager to visit the classroom and ask the children to feedback on their findings. The children could show the work they have produced and decide upon the best pet. This could be decided in the form of a class vote. This can then be continued as the class pet arrives in making sure the class take the best care of the animal you choose together. Make rules about how to look after it, set up a rota of 'pet chores' that need to be completed daily etc.

SESSION 5: THE POST OFFICE

The spark!

Share the thank you card from Appendix 5.4. Detective Della is very happy that we have helped PC Pete to resolve his problems. She has sent us a special certificate (see Appendix 5.5). We are so good at solving problems that she needs our help again. She went to the post office to post our card, and when she arrived the wind had blown a tree down that had broken the window. Everything inside had blown away. The post office had been destroyed.

The children can now discuss:

- What is a post office?

- What is inside?

- What goes on in the post office?

- Who works there (see Appendix 5.6)?

Depending on your children's knowledge, you may like to support their learning through arranging a visit to a local post office. You can also purchase commercially made DVDs that look inside a post office and sorting office. Why not invite a local postman/lady into school to talk to the children. These are useful ways to enhance learning and bring the topic to life.

Let's get creative!

This is the perfect opportunity to set up a class post office. As the children are responsible for its creation, they are more likely to use it purposefully and value its contents.

Prompts

- What does our post office need?

- What do we need to make?

- How are we going to make these items?

- Can we make a list of jobs for the postmaster/mistress to follow?

- Are there any signs that we can make to remind people of what is inside?

- Do we have any rules to help the children use the post office correctly?

Types of activities that may evolve

- Make envelopes, cards, postcards, stamps, money.

- Label items within the post office – stamps, till, scales, parcels.

- Wrap, weigh, order parcels.

- Calculate the cost for purchasing items from the post office.

- Sort letters into the correct initial letter box.

- Complete simple post office forms – making passports, filling in application forms, writing addresses on envelopes, writing and posting letters.

- Role-play post office scenarios.

- Set up a post office role play in your classroom.

Figure 5.14 *Lots of letters to post.*

SESSION 6: THE FIRE STATION

Setting the scene

The children receive an email from PC Pete (see Appendix 5.7). Safetown firefighters have all caught the chickenpox so the fire station has had to close down. PC Pete and Detective Della know very little about being firefighters and need our help.

Time to talk . . .

★ What is a firefighter?

★ What is their job?

★ What do they need to do their job?

★ What do they wear?

★ Do they have special equipment/transport?

★ How do we stay safe against fire?

How can we share these ideas with PC Pete?

Once the children have shared their ideas, this will lead into activities such as . . .

★ Design and make their own fire engines.

★ Make fire equipment – ladders, hoses, cutters, oxygen packs.

★ Make a uniform for them to show the children.

★ Make fire safety rules.

★ Make fire safety posters.

★ List the jobs a firefighter does.

★ Investigate 999 emergency calls.

★ Set up a fire station in the classroom.

★ Write to PC Pete to explain how we can help.

You may like to arrange a visit to the local fire station, where the children can find out more about this topic. The firefighters may share their uniform and equipment, and allow the children to look around the fire engine. This really brings the whole topic to life.

Figure 5.15 *The children made their own fire engines.*

Figure 5.16 *Signs for fire safety.*

Try sharing the children's ideas with PC Pete in a creative way, such as sending him a video message or sending him a fact file or poster all about how to be a super firefighter.

Figure 5.17 *Firefighters' role.*

AND BEYOND . . .

This is a very open-ended project that lends itself to many other problems and scenarios that could be introduced by PC Pete and Detective Della. There is scope to investigate other people who may live in the village, such as:

- Local doctor/nurse

- Dentist

- Mechanic

- Lollipop person

- Optician

- Hairdresser

This topic provides opportunities to invite visitors into your classroom (School Nurse, local mechanic, school lollypop warden etc). Often parents in your school/nursery who are employed in these areas are willing to come in and talk to the children too. You may like to arrange for a local dentist to visit and chat to the children about their tooth cleaning regime or the school nurse to conduct a handwashing workshop.

The types of scenarios you may like to use are . . .

'There is new doctor's surgery being built in the village. PC Pete would like to find out more about what goes on here and help set up the new surgery.'

'PC Pete's police van is still having problems and he needs help to fix it. He needs to visit the mechanic.'

'Detective Della has the toothache and needs help caring for her teeth.'

'There is a busy road near our school and PC Pete is worried about the safety of the children.'

Use the approach and skills you have learned during your time using this project. Remember to let the children lead with their ideas and be creative. If there is a problem, the children will love to help you solve it. Don't be afraid to add in ideas of your own to scaffold the learning, if needed.

These are the types of activities that have evolved during our usage of such scenarios:

- Healthy eating

- Handwashing and germs

- Safe use of medicines

- Roles of the doctor/ nurse

- 999 and what to do in an emergency

- The role of the emergency services

- Tooth care and cleaning

- Road safety

- Wearing a seatbelt in the car

- How to cross the road safely

- Role-playing scenarios

- Setting up a hospital, doctors, optician, etc. in the classroom

ENHANCED PROVISION

- Add simple non-fiction books about each profession into your library.
- Use real-life leaflets into your role play – you can ask your local doctors surgery/dentist to kindly donate a few, if possible.
- Gather real-life equipment to use – rollers, hairbrushes, tools, tyres, washed shampoo/car shampoo bottles, glasses frames, magazines, car manuals, maps, bandages, toothbrushes, etc.

APPENDIX 5.1

EMERGENCY!

Calling all officers . . . help needed immediately.

PC Pete has broken down on the Safetown hills.

As he opened the back door to get his tools out, Donny the sniffer dog slipped his lead and escaped from the van.

Now PC Pete is stranded and Donny is still missing.

PLEASE HELP.

Detective Della

APPENDIX 5.4

Thank you so much

Safetown Police Department

Special detective award

goes to

_____

For solving the mystery of the missing
sniffer dog!

APPENDIX 5.6

Post office

what the children
want to find out

what the children
already know

'What else do you do in
the post office?'
– Suki

'How does the post-
man know where to
take the letters?'
– Rakesh

'You put a stamp on
the front of a letter.'
– Henrietta

'There is a money till
inside and you pay
there.'
– Millie

'What jobs can
you do in there?'
– Nadia

'Why do you put a
stamp on?'
– Jilly

"The postman
works there.'
– Kally

'You put your parcel
on the scales.'
– Kelly

'What is inside a
post office?'
– Daisy

'How do the letters
get to you?'
– Orla

'You post your letters
in a red box.'
– Joe

'The postman puts
the letters in your
letter box.'
– Dylan

'Who works there?'
– Will

'What can you buy
in the post office?'
– Connor

'You can buy cards
and paper there.'
– Esmee

'It is inside a shop, and
you can buy sweets and
food in there as well.'
– Andrea

APPENDIX 5.7

To: _____

From: PoliceOfficerPete@SafetownPolice.com

Date: _____

Dear children,

I have a serious problem that requires your help. There has been an outbreak of chickenpox at the fire station in Safetown and all of the firefighters have come out in spots. They are very contagious, so we have had to close the fire station. If there are any emergencies, there will be no firefighters available to help. Detective Della and I know very little about being a firefighter and wondered if you knew anything about it. Can you help us?

From,

A very worried PC Pete

Developmental band coverage

These are the areas of learning covered by the suggested activities in the book. Remember, your children may suggest other activities, and so this is not an exhaustive checklist.

Personal, social and emotional development

	Making relationships	Self-confidence and self-awareness	Managing feelings and behaviour
22–36 months	• Interested in others' play and starting to join in. • Seeks out others to share experiences.	• Expresses their own preferences and interests.	• Seeks comfort from familiar adults when needed. • Can express their own feelings, such as sad, happy, cross, scared, worried. • Responds to the feelings and wishes of others. • Aware that some actions can hurt or harm others. • Tries to help or give comfort when others are distressed.
30–50 months	• Can play in a group, extending and elaborating play ideas (e.g. building up a role-play activity with other children). • Initiates play, offering cues to peers to join them. • Keeps play going by responding to what others are saying or doing. • Demonstrates friendly behaviour, initiating conversations and forming good relationships with peers and familiar adults.	• Can select and use activities and resources with help. • Welcomes and values praise for what they have done. • Enjoys responsibility of carrying out small tasks. • Is more outgoing towards unfamiliar people and has more confidence in new social situations. • Confident to talk to other children when playing, and will communicate freely. • Shows confidence in asking adults for help.	• Aware of their own feelings, and knows that some actions and words can hurt others' feelings. • Begins to accept the needs of others and can take turns and share resources, sometimes with support from others. • Can usually tolerate delay when needs are not immediately met, and understands wishes may not always be met.
40–60 months	• Initiates conversations, attends to and takes account of what others say. • Explains their own knowledge and understanding, and asks appropriate questions of others.	• Confident to speak to others about their own needs, wants, interests and opinions.	• Understands that their own actions affect other people (e.g. becomes upset or tries to comfort another child when they realise they have upset them). • Beginning to be able to negotiate and solve problems.
ELG	• **Children play cooperatively, taking turns with others. They take account of one another's ideas about how to organise their activity. They show sensitivity to others' needs and feelings.**	• **Children are confident to try new activities, and say why they like some activities more than others. They are confident to speak in a familiar group, will talk about their ideas, and will choose the resources they need for their chosen activities. They say when they do or don't need help.**	• **Children talk about how they and others show feelings, talk about their own and others' behaviour, and its consequences, and know that some behaviour is unacceptable. They work as part of a group or class, and understand and follow the rules.**

Physical development

	Moving and handling	Health and self-care
22–36 months	• Runs safely on whole foot. • Squats with steadiness to rest or play with object on the ground, and rises to feet without using hands. • Climbs confidently and is beginning to pull themselves up on nursery play climbing equipment. • Can kick a large ball. • Turns pages in a book, sometimes several at once. • Shows control in holding and using jugs to pour, hammers, books and mark-making tools. • Beginning to use three fingers (tripod grip) to hold writing tools. • Imitates drawing simple shapes such as circles and lines. • Walks upstairs or downstairs holding on to a rail two feet to a step. • May be beginning to show preference for dominant hand. (These may link into play-based activities and role play.)	• Beginning to recognise danger and seeks support of significant adults for help.
30–50 months	• Moves freely and with pleasure and confidence in a range of ways, such as slithering, shuffling, rolling, crawling, walking, running, jumping, skipping, sliding and hopping. • Mounts stairs, steps or climbing equipment using alternate feet. • Walks downstairs, two feet to each step, while carrying a small object. • Runs skilfully and negotiates space successfully, adjusting speed or direction to avoid obstacles. • Can stand momentarily on one foot when shown. • Can catch a large ball. • Draws lines and circles using gross motor movements. • Uses one-handed tools and equipment (e.g. makes snips in paper with child scissors). • Holds pencil between thumb and two fingers, no longer using whole-hand grasp. • Holds pencil near point between first two fingers and thumb and uses it with good control. • Can copy some letters (e.g. from their name).	• Understands that equipment and tools have to be used safely.
40–60 months	• Experiments with different ways of moving. • Jumps off an object and lands appropriately. • Negotiates space successfully when playing racing and chasing games with other children, adjusting speed or changing direction to avoid obstacles. • Travels with confidence and skill around, under, over and through balancing and climbing equipment. • Uses simple tools to effect changes to materials. • Handles tools, objects, construction and malleable materials safely and with increasing control. • Shows a preference for a dominant hand. • Begins to use anticlockwise movement and retrace vertical lines. • Begins to form recognisable letters. • Uses a pencil and holds it effectively to form recognisable letters, most of which are correctly formed.	• Eats a healthy range of foodstuffs and understands need for variety in food. • Shows some understanding that good practices with regard to exercise, eating, sleeping and hygiene can contribute to good health. • Shows understanding of the need for safety when tackling new challenges, and considers and manages some risks. • Shows understanding of how to transport and store equipment safely. • Shows increasing control over an object in pushing, patting, throwing, catching or kicking it. • Practises some appropriate safety measures without direct supervision.
ELG	• **Children show good control and coordination in large and small movements. They move confidently in a range of ways, safely negotiating space. They handle equipment and tools effectively, including pencils for writing.**	• **Children know the importance for good health of physical exercise, and a healthy diet, and talk about ways to keep healthy and safe.**

Communication and language		
	Listening and attention	**Understanding**	**Speaking**
22–36 months	• Listens with interest to the noises adults make when they read stories. • Single-channelled attention. Can shift to a different task if attention fully obtained.	• Identifies action words by pointing to the right picture (e.g. 'Who's jumping?'). • Understands more complex sentences (e.g. 'Put your toys away and then we'll read a book'). • Understands 'who', 'what', 'where' in simple questions. • Developing understanding of simple concepts (e.g. big/little).	• Uses language as a powerful means of widening contacts and sharing feelings, experiences and thoughts. • Holds a conversation, jumping from topic to topic. • Learns new words very rapidly and is able to use them in communicating. • Uses gestures, sometimes with limited talk (e.g. reaches towards toy, saying 'I have it'). • Uses a variety of questions (e.g. 'what', 'where', 'who'). • Uses simple sentences (e.g. 'Mummy gonna work'). • Beginning to use word endings (e.g. 'going', 'cats').
30–50 months	• Listens to others one to one or in small groups, when conversation interests them. • Listens to stories with increasing attention and recall. • Focusing attention – still listen or do, but can shift their own attention. • Is able to follow directions (if not intently focused on their own choice of activity).	• Understands use of objects (e.g. 'What do we use to cut things?'). • Shows understanding of prepositions such as 'under', 'on top', 'behind' by carrying out an action or selecting correct picture. • Responds to simple instructions (e.g. to get or put away an object). • Beginning to understand 'how' and 'why' questions.	• Beginning to use more complex sentences to link thoughts. • Can retell a simple past event in correct order. • Uses talk to connect ideas, explain what is happening and anticipate what might happen next, recall and relive past experiences. • Questions why things happen and gives explanations (e.g. asks 'who', 'what', 'when', 'how'). • Uses a range of tenses (e.g. 'play', 'playing', 'will play', 'played'). • Uses intonation, rhythm and phrasing to make the meaning clear to others. • Uses vocabulary focused on objects and people that are of particular importance to them. • Builds up vocabulary that reflects the breadth of their experiences. • Uses talk in pretending that objects stand for something else in play (e.g. 'This box is my castle').
40–60 months	• Maintains attention, concentrates and sits quietly during appropriate activity. • Two-channelled attention – can listen and do for short span.	• Responds to instructions involving a two-part sequence. • Able to follow a story without pictures or props. • Listens and responds to ideas expressed by others in conversation or discussion.	• Extends vocabulary, especially by grouping and naming, exploring the meaning and sounds of new words. • Uses language to imagine and recreate roles and experiences in play situations. • Links statements and sticks to a main theme or intention. • Uses talk to organise, sequence and clarify thinking, ideas, feelings and events. • Introduces a storyline or narrative into their play.
ELG	• **Children listen attentively in a range of situations. They listen to stories, accurately anticipating key events and respond to what they hear with relevant comments, questions or actions. They give their attention to what others say and respond appropriately, while engaged in another activity.**	• **Children follow instructions involving several ideas or actions. They answer 'how' and 'why' questions about their experiences and in response to stories or events.**	• **Children express themselves effectively, showing awareness of listeners' needs. They use past, present and future forms accurately when talking about events that have happened or are to happen in the future. They develop their own narratives and explanations by connecting ideas or events.**

Literacy		
	Reading	**Writing**
22–36 months		• Distinguishes between the different marks they make.
30–50 months	• Listens to and joins in with stories and poems, one to one and also in small groups. • Beginning to be aware of the way stories are structured. • Suggests how the story might end. • Listens to stories with increasing attention and recall. • Describes main story settings, events and principal characters. • Shows interest in illustrations and print in books and print in the environment. • Recognises familiar words and signs such as their own name and advertising logos. • Looks at books independently. • Handles books carefully. • Knows information can be relayed in the form of print. • Holds books the correct way up and turns pages. • Knows that print carries meaning and, in English, is read from left to right and top to bottom.	• Sometimes gives meaning to marks as they draw and paint. • Ascribes meaning to marks that they see in different places.
40–60 months	• Hears and says the initial sound in words. • Can segment the sounds in simple words and blend them together and knows which letters represent some of them. • Links sounds to letters, naming and sounding the letters of the alphabet. • Begins to read words and simple sentences. • Uses vocabulary and forms of speech that are increasingly influenced by their experience of books. • Enjoys an increasing range of books. • Knows that information can be retrieved from books and computers.	• Gives meaning to marks they make as they draw, write and paint. • Begins to break the flow of speech into words. • Hears and says the initial sounds in words. • Can segment the sounds in simple words and blend them together. • Links sounds to letters, naming and sounding the letters of the alphabet. • Uses some clearly identifiable letters to communicate meaning, representing some sounds correctly and in sequence. • Writes their own name and other things such as labels, captions. • Attempts to write short sentences in meaningful contexts.
ELG	• **Children read and understand simple sentences. They use phonic knowledge to decode regular words and read them aloud accurately. They also read some common irregular words. They demonstrate understanding when talking with others about what they have read.**	• **Children use their phonic knowledge to write words in ways that match their spoken sounds. They also write some irregular common words. They write simple sentences that can be read by themselves and others. Some words are spelt correctly and others are phonetically plausible.**

Mathematics		
	Numbers	**Shape, space and measures**
22–36 months	• Selects a small number of objects from a group when asked (e.g. 'Please give me one', 'Please give me two'). • Recites some number names in sequence. • Creates and experiments with symbols and marks representing ideas of number. • Begins to make comparisons between quantities. • Uses some language of quantities, such as 'more' and 'a lot'. • Knows that a group of things changes in quantity when something is added or taken away.	• Notices simple shapes and patterns in pictures. • Beginning to categorise objects according to properties such as shape or size. • Begins to use the language of size. • Understands some talk about immediate past and future (e.g. 'before', 'later', 'soon'). • Anticipates specific time-based events such as mealtimes or home time.
30–50 months	• Uses some number names and number language spontaneously. • Uses some number names accurately in play. • Recites numbers in order to 10. • Knows that numbers identify how many objects are in a set. • Beginning to represent numbers using fingers, marks on paper or pictures. • Sometimes matches numeral and quantity correctly. • Shows curiosity about numbers by offering comments or asking questions. • Compares two groups of objects, saying when they have the same number. • Shows an interest in number problems. • Shows an interest in numerals in the environment. • Shows an interest in representing numbers. • Realises not only objects, but anything, can be counted, including steps, claps or jumps.	• Shows an interest in shape and space by playing with shapes or making arrangements with objects. • Shows awareness of similarities of shapes in the environment. • Uses positional language. • Shows interest in shape by sustained construction activity or by talking about shapes or arrangements. • Shows interest in shapes in the environment. • Uses shapes appropriately for tasks. • Beginning to talk about the shapes of everyday objects (e.g. 'round', 'tall').
40–60 months	• Recognises some numerals of personal significance. • Recognises numerals 1 to 5. • Counts up to three or four objects by saying one number name for each item. • Counts actions or objects which cannot be moved. • Counts objects to 10, and beginning to count beyond 10. • Counts out up to six objects from a larger group. • Selects the correct numeral to represent 1 to 5, then 1 to 10, objects. • Counts an irregular arrangement of up to 10 objects. • Estimates how many objects they can see and checks by counting them. • Uses the language of 'more' and 'fewer' to compare two sets of objects. • Finds the total number of items in two groups by counting all of them. • Says the number that is one more than a given number. • Finds one more or one less from a group of up to five objects, then 10 objects. • In practical activities and discussion, beginning to use the vocabulary involved in adding and subtracting. • Records, using marks that they can interpret and explain. • Begins to identify their own mathematical problems based on their own interests and fascinations.	• Beginning to use mathematical names for 'solid' 3D shapes and 'flat' 2D shapes, and mathematical terms to describe shapes. • Selects a particular named shape. • Can describe their relative position such as 'behind' or 'next to'. • Orders two or three items by length or height. • Orders two items by weight or capacity. • Uses familiar objects and common shapes to create and recreate patterns and build models. • Uses everyday language related to time. • Beginning to use everyday language related to money. • Orders and sequences familiar events. • Measures short periods of time in simple ways.
ELG	• **Children count reliably with numbers from 1 to 20, place them in order and say which number is one more or one less that a given number. Using quantities and objects, they add and subtract two single-digit numbers and count on or back to find the answer. They solve problems, including doubling, halving and sharing.**	• **Children use everyday language to talk about size, weight, capacity, position, distance, time and money to compare quantities and objects and to solve problems. They recognise, create and describe patterns. They explore characteristics of everyday objects and shapes and use mathematical language to describe them.**

Understanding the world

	People and communities	The world	Technology
22–36 months	• In pretend play, imitates everyday actions and events from their own family and cultural background (e.g. making and drinking tea). • Learns that they have similarities and differences that connect them to, and distinguish them from, others.	• Enjoys playing with small-world models such as a farm, a garage or a train track.	• Seeks to acquire basic skills in turning on and operating some ICT equipment. • Operates mechanical toys (e.g. turns the knob on a wind-up toy or pulls back on a friction car).
30–50 months	• Shows interest in the lives of people who are familiar to them. • Remembers and talks about significant events in their own experiences. • Recognises and describes special times or events for family or friends. • Shows interest in different occupations and ways of life. • Knows some of the things that make them unique, and can talk about some of the similarities and differences in relation to friends or family.	• Comments and asks questions about aspects of their familiar world, such as the place where they live or the natural world. • Can talk about some of the things they have observed, such as plants, animals, natural and found objects. • Talks about why things happen and how things work. • Developing an understanding of growth, decay and changes over time. • Shows care and concern for living things and the environment.	• Knows how to operate simple equipment (e.g. turns on CD player and uses remote control). • Shows an interest in technological toys with knobs or pulleys, or real objects such as cameras or mobile phones. • Shows skill in making toys work by pressing parts or lifting flaps to achieve effects such as sound, movements or new images. • Knows that information can be retrieved from computers.
40–60 months	• Enjoys joining in with family customs and routines.	• Looks closely at similarities, differences, patterns and change.	• Completes a simple program on a computer. • Uses ICT hardware to interact with age-appropriate computer software.
ELG	• **Children talk about past and present events in their own lives and in the lives of others. They know about similarities and differences between themselves and others, and among families, communities and traditions.**	• **Children know about similarities and differences in relation to places, objects, materials and living things. They talk about the features of their own immediate environment and how environments might vary from one another. They make observation of animals and plants and explain why some things occur, and talk about changes.**	• **Children recognise that a range of technology is used in places such as homes and schools. They select and use technology for particular purposes.**

Expressive Arts and Design

	Media and materials	Being imaginative
22–36 months	• Creates sounds by banging, shaking, tapping or blowing. • Shows an interest in the way musical instruments sound. • Experiments with blocks, colours and marks.	• Beginning to use representation to communicate (e.g. drawing a line and saying 'That's me'). • Beginning to make-believe by pretending.
30–50 months	• Enjoys joining in with dancing and ring games. • Beginning to move rhythmically. • Imitates movement in response to music. • Explores and learns how sounds can be changed. • Explores colour and how colours can be changed. • Understands that they can use lines to enclose a space, and then begin to use these shapes to represent objects. • Beginning to be interested in and describe the texture of things. • Uses various construction materials. • Beginning to construct, stacking blocks vertically and horizontally, making enclosures and creating spaces. • Joins construction pieces together to build and balance. • Realises tools can be used for a purpose.	• Developing preferences for forms of expression. • Uses movement to express feelings. • Creates movement in response to music. • Sings to self and makes up simple songs. • Makes up rhythms. • Notices what adults do, imitating what is observed and then doing it spontaneously when the adult is not there. • Engages in imaginative role play based on their own first-hand experiences. • Builds stories around toys (e.g. farm animals needing rescue from an armchair 'cliff'). • Uses available resources to create props to support role play. • Captures experiences and responses with a range of media, such as music, dance and paint and other materials or words.
40–60 months	• Explores the different sounds of instruments. • Explores what happens when they mix colours. • Experiments to create different textures. • Understands that different media can be combined to create new effects. • Manipulates materials to achieve a planned effect. • Constructs with a purpose in mind, using a variety of resources. • Uses simple tools and techniques competently and appropriately. • Selects appropriate resources and adapts work where necessary. • Selects tools and techniques needed to shape, assemble and join materials they are using.	• Creates simple representations of events, people and objects. • Initiates new combinations of movement and gesture in order to express and respond to feelings, ideas and experiences. • Chooses particular colours to use for a purpose. • Introduces a storyline or narrative into their play. • Plays alongside other children who are engaged in the same theme. • Plays cooperatively as part of a group to develop and act out a narrative.
ELG	• **Children sing songs, make music and dance, and experiment with ways of changing them. They safely use and explore a variety of materials, tools and techniques, experimenting with colour, design, texture, form and function.**	• **Children use what they have learnt about media and materials in original ways, thinking about uses and purposes. They represent their own ideas, thoughts and feelings through design and technology, art, music, dance, role play and stories.**

Resources

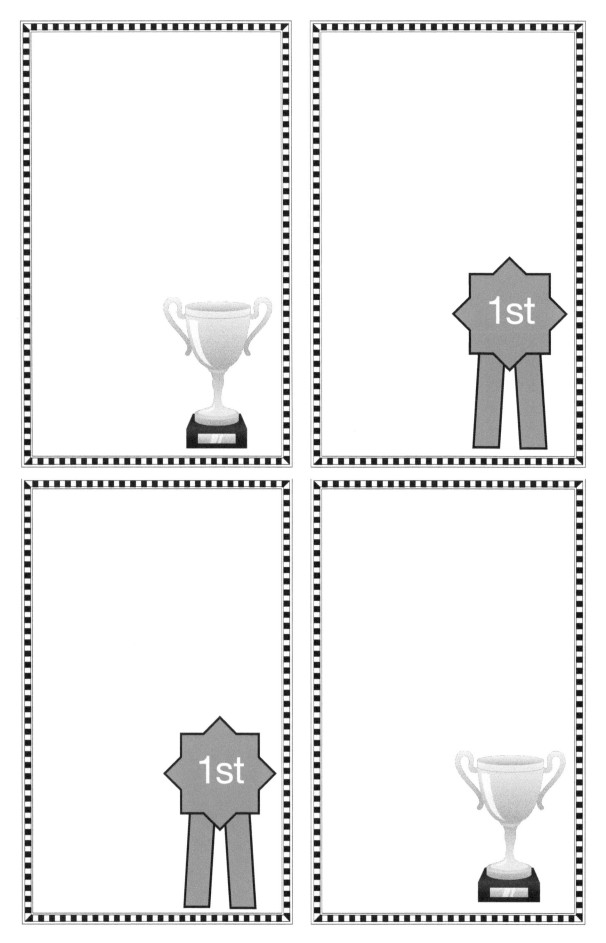

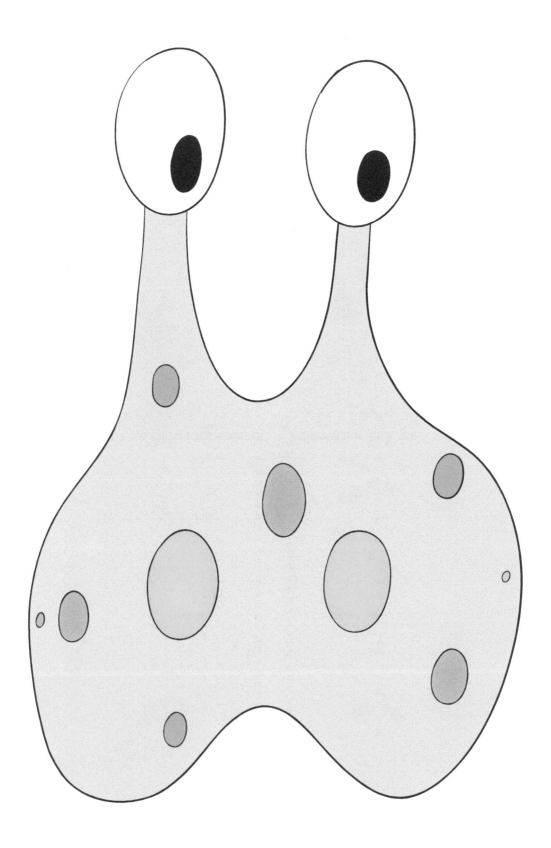

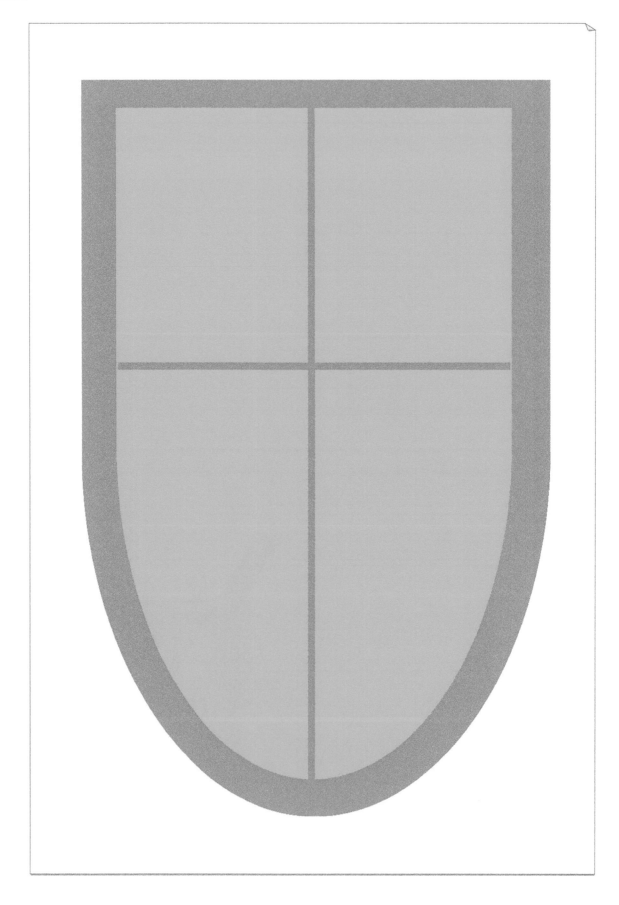

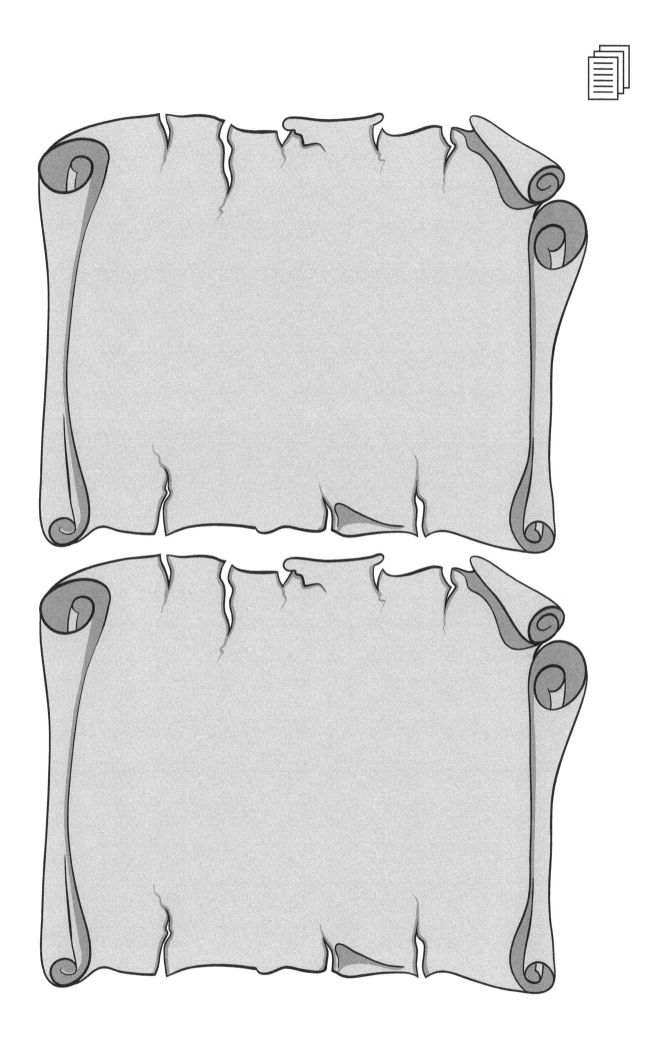

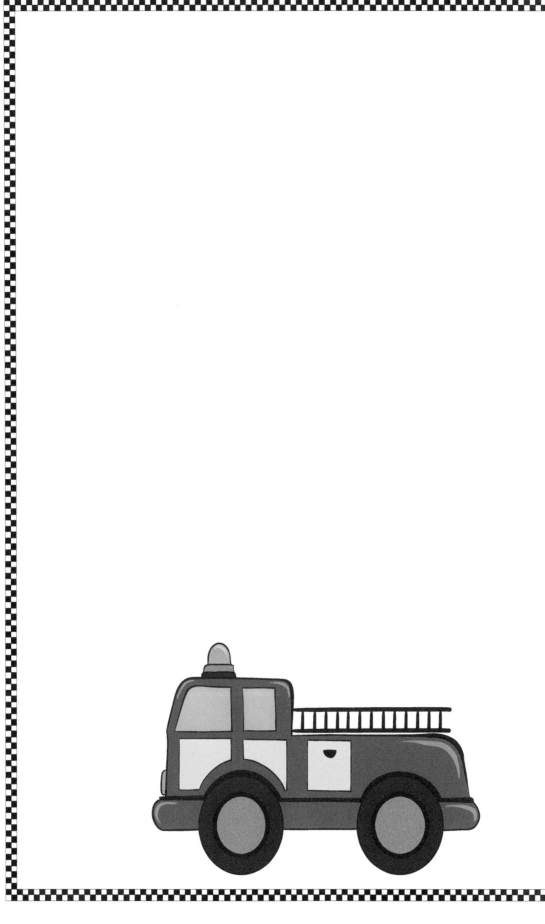

Tally Chart

Pictogram

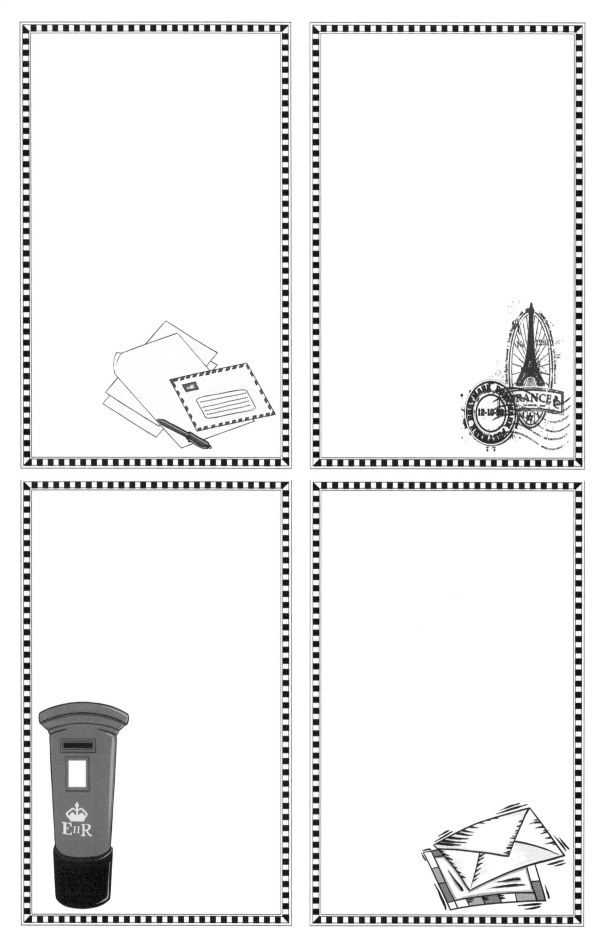